SEX WITH STRANGERS

BY LAURA EASON

★

DRAMATISTS
PLAY SERVICE
INC.

SEX WITH STRANGERS was first produced in a developmental production by Steppenwolf Theatre Company (Martha Lavey, Artistic Director; David Hawkanson, Executive Director) in Chicago, Illinois, as part of its First Look Repertory of New Work (Edward Sobel, Program Director) in July – August 2009. It was directed by Jessica Thebus. The cast was as follows:

OLIVIA ....Amy J. Carle
ETHAN.. Stephen Louis Grush

The world premiere of a revised version of SEX WITH STRANGERS opened at Steppenwolf Theatre Company on January 30, 2011. It was directed by Jessica Thebus; the set design was by Todd Rosenthal; the lighting design was by J.R. Lederle; the costume design was by Ana Kuzmanic; the sound design and original music were by Kevin O'Donnell and Andre Pluess; the production stage manager was Christine D. Freeburg; and the dramaturg was Polly Carl. The cast was as follows:

OLIVIA ....Sally Murphy
ETHAN.. Stephen Louis Grush

The Australian premiere of a revised version of SEX WITH STRANGERS opened at Sydney Theatre Company (Cate Blanchett and Andrew Upton, Artistic Directors) in Sydney, Australia, on September 28, 2012. It was directed by Jocelyn Moorhouse; the set and costume design were by Tracy Grant Lord; the lighting design was by Matthew Marshall; the original music and sound design were by Steve Francis; the production stage manager was Tanya Leach; and the voice and text coach was Charmian Gradwell. The cast was as follows:

OLIVIA .... Jacqueline McKenzie
ETHAN... Ryan Corr

The New York premiere of a revised version of SEX WITH STRANGERS opened at Second Stage Theatre (Carole Rothman, Artistic Director; Casey Reitz, Executive Director) in New York City on July 30, 2014. It was directed by David Schwimmer; the assistant director was J. Nicole Brooks; the set design was by Andromache Chalfant; the costume design was by ESosa; the lighting design was by Japhy Weideman; the original music and sound design were by Fitz Patton; and the production stage manager was Scott Taylor Rollison. The cast was as follows:

OLIVIA .... Anna Gunn
ETHAN... Billy Magnussen

CHARACTERS

OLIVIA, 39, then 41. Smart, sexy, outwardly strong but covering some fragility. American but spent many years living abroad.

ETHAN, 28, then 30. Very charismatic, sexy, a fast talker, used to being the center of attention. From Chicago but has little to no specific accent.

PLACE

Act One: A bed and breakfast in rural Michigan.

Act Two: Olivia's apartment in Chicago.

TIME

The present.

TEXT NOTES

[//] An interruption, where the following line of dialogue should begin.
[...] A suspended thought.
[—] A cut off.

SEX WITH STRANGERS

ACT ONE

Scene 1

The living/reading room of a simple, not overly quaint bed and breakfast. A window looks out on the late, cold, snowy March night. There is a fire going. Next to the couch is a tall stack of books.

Holding a red pen in one hand and a glass of red wine in the other, Olivia sits reading an unbound manuscript. She occasionally makes notes and is happily alone.

The sound of a car approaching. As headlights come into view, Olivia looks curiously out the window.

OLIVIA. *(Re: the car out the window.)* Who are you? *(The sound of the car engine turning off, someone approaching the house. They turn the knob but the door is locked. To the door.)* Hello?

ETHAN. *(Through the door.)* Hey — I'm Ethan Kane. I have a reservation.

OLIVIA. What?

ETHAN. *(Through the door.)* I have a reservation.

OLIVIA. *(To herself.)* You have got to be kidding. *(To the door.)* OK. One second. *(Olivia looks for her sweater. It takes a second.)*

ETHAN. Uh, it's really cold out here.

OLIVIA. I'm coming! *(Olivia puts on her sweater and opens the door. Ethan blows past her into the room, making wet footprints. He throws his coat down on the floor.)*

ETHAN. Hi.

OLIVIA. Sorry, but Anne's not here. She didn't think you were coming. Check-in was between noon and six.

ETHAN. Yeah. I got a late start. And, in case you didn't notice, it's a fucking blizzard out there.

OLIVIA. Well, she didn't leave you a room key. So …

ETHAN. OK. *(Dropping his bag by the couch.)* Well, I'll just crash here.

OLIVIA. On the couch?

ETHAN. Yeah. What do you want me to do? Sleep in the car?

OLIVIA. No. I wasn't // suggesting you —

ETHAN. Is there food?

OLIVIA. Food?

ETHAN. Yeah, I'm starving. There's got to be something in the kitchen.

OLIVIA. I don't think you should be rooting around in the kitchen —

ETHAN. You're really rule-oriented, huh?

OLIVIA. No. I just don't // think you should —

ETHAN. *(Pointing to her open bottle of wine.)* Did you buy that bottle of wine?

OLIVIA. I'll tell Anne I drank it and she'll charge it to my bill.

ETHAN. So, she can charge what I eat to mine. This way? *(Ethan goes to the kitchen. Olivia collects her manuscript.)*

OLIVIA. *(To herself.)* What a jag-off!

ETHAN. *(Calling.)* You want anything?

OLIVIA. *(Calling.)* No, thanks.

ETHAN. *(Calling.)* Am I seeming like a dick?

OLIVIA. *(To herself.)* What?!

ETHAN. *(Calling, louder.)* Hey — am I seeming like a dick?

OLIVIA. *(Calling.)* Yeah. Yeah, you are.

ETHAN. *(After a beat, calling.)* Sorry. Hungry. Man, I got so lost coming here! Once you get off the highway, there are no street lights *anywhere*, half the signs I couldn't see, and with the snow, I was like, where the fuck am I?!

OLIVIA. That's why they tell you to get here before six. *(Ethan returns with a bowl of cereal and an empty juice glass.)*

ETHAN. Smart.

OLIVIA. Um, I should head to bed.

ETHAN. You don't seem tired.

OLIVIA. Well …

ETHAN. I think it's all that rage you're barely suppressing.

OLIVIA. *(Smiling in spite of herself.)* I thought I was managing it pretty well.

ETHAN. Stay for a minute.

OLIVIA. No. I should get some sleep.

ETHAN. *(Holding out his empty glass.)* You sharing or…?

OLIVIA. I don't really want to.

ETHAN. C'mon. You can bill my glass to the couch.

OLIVIA. *(After a moment of consideration.)* All right. *(Olivia fills Ethan's glass.)*

ETHAN. So, you've been here before?

OLIVIA. Yes.

ETHAN. *(Laughing.)* And…?

OLIVIA. And yes. I've been here before.

ETHAN. Are you usually this easy to talk to or…?

OLIVIA. Who *are* you?

ETHAN. What?

OLIVIA. *Who are you?* Why are you here?

ETHAN. Is it weird that I'm here?

OLIVIA. Yes!

ETHAN. Why?

OLIVIA. You're not the kind of guy who usually comes here — How do you even know about this place?

ETHAN. A friend of mine's been here. Said it was great. *(Fiddling with his iPhone.)* I'm on a deadline and I'm really distracted at home and he thought I could get some work done here so — *(Looking at his phone.)* I have no signal. Do you get signal here?

OLIVIA. No.

ETHAN. Never?

OLIVIA. Never.

ETHAN. Seriously? *(Looking to his phone.)* Shit!

OLIVIA. Is someone trying to get a hold of you?

ETHAN. It's not about someone trying to get a hold of me …

OLIVIA. There's a phone if you have to make a call.

ETHAN. It's not that I have to make a call, but, I mean, *my phone isn't working*!

OLIVIA. *(Mocking him.)* Are you gonna be OK?

ETHAN. *(Frustrated, waving his iPhone.)* I can't find the wireless. She said there was wireless.

OLIVIA. It's down.

ETHAN. What? It's, like, broken?

OLIVIA. Yes.

ETHAN. So, can I plug in somewhere?

OLIVIA. No. Something's wrong with the line. Someone was supposed to come fix it in the next day or two, but with the storm …

ETHAN. So, no internet at all?

OLIVIA. Nope.

ETHAN. Fuck!

OLIVIA. It's been great, actually. No distractions.

ETHAN. But *I can't get online*! People will think I'm dead. And what if you have to look something up?

OLIVIA. I don't.

ETHAN. But what if you need to know something?

OLIVIA. What would I need to know that urgently?

ETHAN. I don't know. *(Looking to his phone.)* Anything …

OLIVIA. No matter how many times you look at it, you're not going to get a signal.

ETHAN. Shit!

OLIVIA. How long are you planning on staying?

ETHAN. If there's no wireless … I mean, *I* have to look stuff up.

OLIVIA. Probably best you leave in the morning then.

ETHAN. *(Laughing at her harshness.)* OK.

OLIVIA. I'm just thinking of you.

ETHAN. Well, I'm not going anywhere tonight. *(As he talks, Ethan pockets his phone, looks around for the bathroom.)* God, it took so long to get here. My friend was like, "It's a couple of hours," and I was like, Michigan, OK, sure. *(He goes offstage into the unseen bathroom and starts peeing.)*

OLIVIA. You drove from Chicago?

ETHAN. *(Offstage.)* Yeah, and it took forever with all the ice. When is this going to stop? It's *March*.

OLIVIA. *(Re: the sound of his peeing.)* Could you close the door?

ETHAN. *(Offstage.)* Sorry. *(Ethan closes the door. Calling through the door.)* Shouldn't we be by the lake? *(Toilet flushes. Ethan comes out of the bathroom. He takes out his phone again.)* Why come all the way out here to not be by the lake?

OLIVIA. It's more built-up near the lake. Here, it's quiet so people can write.

ETHAN. *(Looking to his phone.)* Right.

OLIVIA. Jesus, you can't stop.

ETHAN. Yes. I can. *(Ethan puts down his iPhone. He refills his now-empty glass, then holds out the wine bottle to Olivia.)*

OLIVIA. *(After a quick moment of consideration.)* Why not? *(He pours. They drink.)*

ETHAN. *(Looking at her manuscript.)* What are you working on? Looks like you're proofing.

OLIVIA. Yeah.

ETHAN. A book?

OLIVIA. A novel. But I'm … I'm more of a *hobbyist*.

ETHAN. What does that mean?

OLIVIA. I don't do it professionally.

ETHAN. No?

OLIVIA. No.

ETHAN. So, what do you do? Professionally.

OLIVIA. I teach.

ETHAN. Isn't it a schoolnight?

OLIVIA. Spring break.

ETHAN. *(Teasing her.)* Wow, you're really getting crazy, huh?

OLIVIA. *(Teasing back.)* Don't feel any pressure to keep up.

ETHAN. *(Looking around.)* I was afraid this place'd be lame, "quaint" or something, but it's not too bad.

OLIVIA. When's your deadline?

ETHAN. Last week.

OLIVIA. Oh, no.

ETHAN. Yeah, so, I have to finish by Friday.

OLIVIA. Is that possible?

ETHAN. It has to be. My friend Ahmit says this place was like magic for him so —

OLIVIA. Ahmit? Ahmit Faulk?

ETHAN. Yeah.

OLIVIA. You know Ahmit Faulk?

ETHAN. Yeah. I took a master class with him last year and now he's a buddy of mine.

OLIVIA. He and I were in school together. I told him about this place, actually. I brought him here.

ETHAN. Right. You're Olivia Lago.

OLIVIA. *(Slowly.)* Uh, yeah. I am.

ETHAN. When Ahmit told me about this place, he said you used to come here. I've, uh, I've read your book.

OLIVIA. No, you haven't.

ETHAN. I have.

OLIVIA. How? It's out of print.

ETHAN. Ahmit gave it to me.

OLIVIA. What do you mean?

ETHAN. I was asking him about writers that he loved and he gave it to me. Said it was one of his favorites.

OLIVIA. No. He didn't.

ETHAN. Why do you sound so shocked?

OLIVIA. I haven't seen him in a long time, since before he won the Pulitzer. I had no idea that he ... He said my book was one of his favorites?

ETHAN. He did.

OLIVIA. *(Taking that in. Then ...)* He never told me that.

ETHAN. And I love it, too.

OLIVIA. You really read it?

ETHAN. Twice! And I don't read anything twice. I started over right after I read the last page. I was, like, possessed by it.

OLIVIA. Uh ... Wow. Thank you.

ETHAN. I actually, when I called, I asked the woman —

OLIVIA. Anne?

ETHAN. Yeah, I asked her if you still came here.

OLIVIA. What did she say?

ETHAN. She said you did. She said you were here, actually.

OLIVIA. *(Slowly, realizing he sought her out.)* Oh. *(They drink.)*

ETHAN. So, what happened?

OLIVIA. What? With Ahmit and me?

ETHAN. *(With a smile at her question.)* No. With your writing.

OLIVIA. Oh. Well. Not much, obviously.

ETHAN. That freaks me out.

OLIVIA. Why?

ETHAN. Something more should have happened.

OLIVIA. Yeah, well ... that's the story sometimes.

ETHAN. So, the book came out and...?

OLIVIA. Why are you so interested?

ETHAN. Why don't you want to talk about it?

OLIVIA. It's not that I don't want to talk about it. It just feels, I don't know, personal somehow.

ETHAN. That doesn't mean you can't tell me.

OLIVIA. OK.

ETHAN. So?

OLIVIA. Well …

ETHAN. Come on.

OLIVIA. It just didn't do very well.

ETHAN. In what way?

OLIVIA. Well, the reviews were mixed, which didn't generate the kind of, whatever, *excitement* everyone hoped for and sales were disappointing. So, my publisher and I parted ways. And, because of that, my agent and I parted ways …

ETHAN. What did the reviews say?

OLIVIA. I don't really remember.

ETHAN. *(Calling her out.)* That is such a lie.

OLIVIA. *(Smiling at his calling her out.)* I don't remember every word like I used to.

ETHAN. Who liked it?

OLIVIA. He's gone now, but Ed Christiansen at the *Trib*, not the lead but smart, well-respected. And a couple others. But most people didn't get it.

ETHAN. Why?

OLIVIA. Well, it was the late '90s … *(Cringing.)* And the cover … it was this fashion-y looking woman in pointy pumps loaded down with *shopping bags*.

ETHAN. Yeah, it was *bad*. I never would have read it in a hundred million years if Ahmit didn't basically force me.

OLIVIA. My publisher thought jumping on the "chick-lit" band-wagon was a good idea. But the people who would have liked it didn't buy it because of what they thought it was. And the people who did buy it hated it because it wasn't what they expected. It was a disaster.

ETHAN. Brutal.

OLIVIA. And, honestly, I thought the book was great.

ETHAN. It *is* great!

OLIVIA. So when it was misunderstood or, even with a few good reviews, basically dismissed … it was pretty devastating.

ETHAN. So, what then? You stopped writing?!

OLIVIA. No. I got back on the horse, wrote another book and tried to get it out there but … I wrote it with something to prove which is never the best place to come from.

ETHAN. Yeah.

OLIVIA. No one wanted it — no one who I thought deserved it, anyway. So after that, I stopped. For a long time.

ETHAN. You stopped trying?

OLIVIA. I don't know what to tell you. *I got discouraged.*

ETHAN. So. We all get discouraged.

OLIVIA. Do you get paid to write?

ETHAN. Yeah.

OLIVIA. So, you're also getting some encouragement.

ETHAN. But you should see the shit people, especially critics, have said about me! I have a couple of books out and they've done pretty well —

OLIVIA. That's great.

ETHAN. Yeah, but it all started from this blog I used to write. And critics think that a book based on a blog is the lowest form of literature, "one step above catalogues and fortune cookies"!

OLIVIA. Did someone actually say that?

ETHAN. Yes! People say totally horrifying things about me — to me! — all the time. People also say crazy, hero-worship shit. I don't listen to any of it. All those chumps are just jealous I was on the Best Seller list.

OLIVIA. The Best Seller list?

ETHAN. Yeah.

OLIVIA. Which Best Seller list?

ETHAN. The, uh, the *New York Times* Best Seller list.

OLIVIA. *The New York Times Best Seller list?*

ETHAN. Yeah.

OLIVIA. *(Incredulous.)* No.

ETHAN. Yeah.

OLIVIA. Really?

ETHAN. Don't you wish you could look it up?

OLIVIA. The *New York Times* Best Seller list?

ETHAN. Yeah. For five years.

OLIVIA. *Five years?!*

ETHAN. Counting both books. Yeah. Paperback non-fiction, but *still*, especially since it was mostly guys my age, early/mid-twenties, and a lot of college kids. Which is why they wanted to do the book in the first place. The blog was getting over a million hits a month, mostly from people under twenty-five —

OLIVIA. *(Amazed.)* A million people a month?

ETHAN. Hits, but yeah. The tasteless youth of the world put me on the Best Seller list! And that's why critics don't like me. They all want to be king-makers, hanging on to their last bit of power before their papers go under. But they don't really matter anymore. I got totally mixed reviews and I was on the Best Seller list for five years!

OLIVIA. Wait — what's your name again?

ETHAN. Ethan Kane. But I publish under the name Ethan Strange.

OLIVIA. *(Name ringing a bell.)* Yeah.

ETHAN. And even though I've been off the list for a year or so, the books are still selling great.

OLIVIA. What are they called?

ETHAN. *Sex with Strangers* is the first one.

OLIVIA. *(Ringing a bell.)* Yeah. *(Realizing.)* I've seen it at the airport!

ETHAN. We actually sell a lot of copies at the airport.

OLIVIA. So, is that what it's about? Having sex with strangers?

ETHAN. Yeah.

OLIVIA. Is it porn?

ETHAN. No, it's not porn.

OLIVIA. It sounds like porn.

ETHAN. It's not like *porn* porn. It started because I had this blog, but just a "I'm nineteen and want to be a writer so read this" bullshit blog. But I wrote this kind-of funny story about this girl I met at a bar and how I ended up doing all this crazy shit to get her to have sex with me, but she wouldn't. My friends were like, yeah, girls won't fuck guys they just meet in bars anymore, because everyone meets online, pre-screens, you know? Even though half of what people say about themselves is bullshit. Anyway, I said in-person still works if you can talk, most people just can't, or, not like I can. So, I bet my friends I could have sex with a stranger every week for a year. But the deal was, I had to go out to bars or wherever and meet girls the old-fashioned way, stranger to stranger. So, I started a blog about that.

OLIVIA. So, is it really non-fiction?

ETHAN. We call the book "an internet memoir based on the intoxicated recollections of a certifiable asshole."

OLIVIA. What does *that* mean?

ETHAN. Well, I drink a lot. And, sometimes, I can't remember what the fuck happened. So, you know, I filled in some blanks, and maybe some things are exaggerated for the sake of a good story. But with that title, we covered our asses.

OLIVIA. OK.

ETHAN. The whole thing was actually much harder than I thought it'd be.

OLIVIA. *(With mock pity.)* Awwww …

ETHAN. But, finally, I ended up fucking this girl that had a really popular site and she linked to me when I wrote, in *awe*, about the fact that, in addition to being, like, crazy flexible, she could shoot, you know, shoot —

OLIVIA. OK.

ETHAN. — out of her pussy! —

OLIVIA. Got it!

ETHAN. Anyway, it was really funny. And after that I started getting a lot of hits and people got to know where I would hang out and then it was pretty easy since girls wanted to be written about in the blog.

OLIVIA. Girls slept with you to get written about in a *blog*?

ETHAN. I like to think that's not the only reason.

OLIVIA. No, I, uh, I get it.

ETHAN. Some girl even started an "I Fucked Ethan Strange" blog — she started the Ethan *Strange* thing. I was just plain Ethan Kane before that.

OLIVIA. How is this not porn?

ETHAN. No pictures. So anyway, when a girl fucked me, it became this *thing* …

OLIVIA. What? That they'd *brag* about?

ETHAN. Blog about.

OLIVIA. This is fascinating.

ETHAN. And this online sort-of club formed by girls who'd had sex with me —

OLIVIA. Come on. You're making this up.

ETHAN. I'd show you the site if I could.

OLIVIA. So, what? They all wrote about having sex with you?

ETHAN. They wrote about what I wrote about having sex with them and, you know, where they think I got it wrong or whatever.

OLIVIA. Do you still see any of these fifty-two girls?

ETHAN. I actually ended up doing little better than that. But, no, not as much as I used to. I usually hang out at this one bar and sometimes they still come around.

OLIVIA. So, you hang out in bars with a bunch of girls you've slept with, and they all know they've slept with you and have read about each other sleeping with you…?

ETHAN. And some of them have slept with each other.

OLIVIA. And wrote about it?

ETHAN. Yeah, some of 'em.

OLIVIA. That's *crazy* to me. Isn't there anything you want to keep private?

ETHAN. I guess not.

OLIVIA. I just wouldn't want certain things, most things, especially sexual things about me available to the random stranger.

ETHAN. Clearly, I don't mind.

OLIVIA. I do get it *generally* — not all the documentation — but having sex with strangers can be good. No expectations, no disappointments.

ETHAN. Yeah, but what about the upside of seeing someone again? If you like them and have fun, you get to bring that back.

OLIVIA. Shouldn't you be selling me on strangers?

ETHAN. I don't know, should I? *(A moment as that hangs in the air. They drink.)* Anyway, the second book came out a couple years ago …

OLIVIA. *(Re: the title.) More Sex with Strangers?*

ETHAN. Yes, actually. Did great. Sold a lot. *Times* Best Seller list. Et cetera. I was ready to move on. But then the first book got optioned to be a movie, so —

OLIVIA. You're turning that book into a movie?

ETHAN. Yeah.

OLIVIA. *(Teasing.)* Is *that* going to be porn?

ETHAN. Shut up.

OLIVIA. I'm just asking.

ETHAN. That's what I'm behind on, the screenplay I have to finish. So, it's cool, but I'm moving on to other things.

OLIVIA. Yeah?

ETHAN. I won't be the "*Sex with Strangers* guy" forever, writing like this when I'm, like … *(He gestures towards her.)* Forty or whatever.

OLIVIA. *(With a smile.)* I'm not forty.

ETHAN. I just mean, you're not going to find me, you know, years from now doing the convention circuit, signing copies of *The Sex with Strangers Guide to Sex Over Sixty.* I mean, fucking shoot me.

OLIVIA. OK.

ETHAN. All of that is going to be a stepping stone.

OLIVIA. To what?

ETHAN. Among other things, I, uh, I have a novel I've been working on.

OLIVIA. You wrote a novel?

ETHAN. Don't sound so surprised!

OLIVIA. *(She is.)* I'm not.

ETHAN. I've been working on it, on and off, for a while, so once the movie's over ... *(Back to his point.)* Anyway, all that to say, sex with strangers is basically done.

OLIVIA. Basically?

ETHAN. Yeah. I mean, sure, every now and then ...

OLIVIA. Sure.

ETHAN. Hey — at least I'm not fucking over any poor people in third-world countries or robbing anyone's life savings or whatever. I mean, I'm one of the good guys, *relatively*, just trying to make a living without selling my soul.

OLIVIA. You are so right! You're kind-of a modern day Mother Teresa! But instead of *helping* poor strangers, you have sex with them!

ETHAN. I do what I can. *(Looking to her manuscript.)* So, let me read your new book.

OLIVIA. What? No.

ETHAN. Come on.

OLIVIA. No.

ETHAN. Why not?

OLIVIA. Why do you want to?

ETHAN. Self-explanatory.

OLIVIA. Thanks. But no.

ETHAN. Why not?

OLIVIA. I don't know you at all.

ETHAN. If that's your criteria, no wonder things have stalled out for you. It's finished, isn't it?

OLIVIA. Mostly. There are a few things ...

ETHAN. Let me read it.

OLIVIA. Sorry.

ETHAN. Come on!

OLIVIA. No.

ETHAN. Really?

OLIVIA. *(Just looks at him.)* ...

ETHAN. OK. OK. *(After a moment.)* So, what do you do around here for fun?

OLIVIA. People come here to write, not to have fun.

ETHAN. Let's watch a movie.

OLIVIA. Sadly, no TV.

ETHAN. Seriously?

OLIVIA. Seriously. Uh ... cards?

ETHAN. Sure. Are there some?

OLIVIA. *(Looking around.)* I don't think so.

ETHAN. We could download a — oh, no we can't! We can't do anything! Well ... actually ... there is one thing we could do.

OLIVIA. Are you making a pass at me?

ETHAN. Yeah. I am.

OLIVIA. Don't do that!

ETHAN. Why not?

OLIVIA. You're a total stranger! You literally just walked in off the street.

ETHAN. I thought that was all right with you.

OLIVIA. Well ... not ... // I mean —

ETHAN. OK. You seemed ... OK.

OLIVIA. Seemed what?

ETHAN. Seemed into me.

OLIVIA. What?!

ETHAN. You did.

OLIVIA. I didn't.

ETHAN. You did.

OLIVIA. What did I...?

ETHAN. It's fine. You're into it or you're not.

OLIVIA. I don't know you at *all*.

ETHAN. I thought you were cool with that.

OLIVIA. I am. But why would I sleep with *you*? So you can write about me? No, thanks.

ETHAN. I wouldn't.

OLIVIA. Why should I trust you?

ETHAN. You probably shouldn't.

OLIVIA. You seem like you might be an asshole.

ETHAN. I'm not saying I'm not an asshole. I pretty much *am* an asshole. I'm just saying I won't be an asshole to you.

OLIVIA. OK...?

ETHAN. I'm only an asshole to people who are assholes. The world is just really, really full of assholes.

OLIVIA. Oh, I know.

ETHAN. And I like you. A lot.

OLIVIA. You've known me for ten minutes.

ETHAN. *(Moving in on her.)* I've been inside your head.

OLIVIA. Oh, please. My book was fiction, not like yours.

19

ETHAN. How many people do you think you're close to?

OLIVIA. What?!

ETHAN. I bet I get you more than ninety-five percent of them.

OLIVIA. That is an arrogant thing to say.

ETHAN. I think you're brilliant. If I could write like you … *(A beat.)* "I felt like a ruined city … "

OLIVIA. What are you…?

ETHAN. "I felt like a ruined city … whose loss will be built over and forgotten."

OLIVIA. Are you *quoting* me?

ETHAN. I am fucking quoting you. *(Ethan kisses her. Passionately. She kisses him back. Passionately. Clothes begin to come off. Sex is imminent.)*

Scene 2

Late the next morning. Snow continues to fall outside. Olivia is cleaning up a stack of books that were knocked over the night before. Ethan enters from the bedroom.

ETHAN. Hey.

OLIVIA. *(Overly casual.)* Hey.

ETHAN. Still snowing?

OLIVIA. Yeah.

ETHAN. *(Re: her cleaning up.)* Is someone else coming?

OLIVIA. No. Anne called and everyone else cancelled because of the snow. I'm just cleaning up.

ETHAN. So, it's just us.

OLIVIA. Just me, officially. Anne asked if I could take care of the place while she checks on her Dad up in Mackinaw. I didn't mention you were here.

ETHAN. No?

OLIVIA. Since you're not staying.

ETHAN. Right. So … last night was pretty great.

OLIVIA. Oh. Don't. I hate to reminisce about sex.

ETHAN. That's just about all I do. Have sex and reminisce about it. *(Re: the books.)* What are all of those?

OLIVIA. They're mine.

ETHAN. You can read all of these in a week?

OLIVIA. No. I always bring more than I can possibly read, including favorites to reread, which I never get to. I just like having them around, I guess, knowing they're close by.

ETHAN. *(Picking up an old hardcover.)* This one's old, huh?

OLIVIA. First edition.

ETHAN. *(Smelling the book.)* This smells like a library to me.

OLIVIA. How's that?

ETHAN. *(Smelling the book.)* Like old paper … and use … and time …

OLIVIA. *(Smelling the book.)* Old books … best smell in the world.

ETHAN. *(Picking up a copy of* The Lover *by Marguerite Duras.)* How's this?

OLIVIA. You never read it?

ETHAN. Nope.

OLIVIA. But you've heard of her.

ETHAN. Maybe? Marguerite … *(Mispronouncing the name.)* Der-us?

OLIVIA. *(Gently correcting the pronunciation.)* Duras.

ETHAN. I'm a little behind, honestly.

OLIVIA. I'm guessing not many nights at home curled up with a book.

ETHAN. Not many nights at home.

OLIVIA. I find this so strange. I see it with my students all the time. Writers who don't read.

ETHAN. I read. Constantly.

OLIVIA. More than a hundred and forty characters at a time.

ETHAN. *(Quickly.)* I *do* read. But mostly living writers. I'm good on the big guns — Eggers, Franzen, Zadie Smith. But also who's next. So, yeah, I'm a little behind on some of the *dead* people. But I'm committed to catching up.

OLIVIA. *(Impressed.)* Nice.

ETHAN. *(Re: the book.)* What do you like about this?

OLIVIA. Well, I was nineteen when I first read it and totally devotional to it, so I'm not very objective. But it's the way she uses language — it's very spare, but incredibly vivid.

ETHAN. Yeah?

OLIVIA. The way she evokes the feeling of desire, of passion, of feeling inexplicably connected to another person … what happens before words are even spoken and, then, later, when you don't need them anymore. And I know it's a cliché but there is something about passion and the French.

ETHAN. Ahmit said you lived in France for a long time?

OLIVIA. Did you ask him about me?

ETHAN. I did. I wanted to know everything about you.

OLIVIA. Just from reading my book?

ETHAN. Yeah. And I saw a picture of you.

OLIVIA. You did? Where?

ETHAN. Your book jacket.

OLIVIA. Right.

ETHAN. But also on Facebook.

OLIVIA. I'm not on Facebook anymore.

ETHAN. Ahmit posted a photo of your class or something.

OLIVIA. *(Really horrified.)* Oh, God. What photo?

ETHAN. *(Re: what she was wearing.)* Red pants.

OLIVIA. *(Concerned.)* Oh no. *(After a beat of reflection.)* Actually, I looked good in those pants.

ETHAN. You did. When I saw you, I thought, she wrote that unbelievable book and she looks like that?

OLIVIA. *(Smiling.)* OK …

ETHAN. I looked you up. But there's basically nothing.

OLIVIA. I guess I'm the last anonymous person in my generation.

ETHAN. How long were you there? In France?

OLIVIA. In Europe for eight. In Paris, but also Rome and Barcelona.

ETHAN. Why did you ever come back?

OLIVIA. I went for love. And it ended.

ETHAN. What happened?

OLIVIA. He was Italian. Very handsome. Older than me. He traveled for work and so I really didn't. Work. But I saw the world and learned languages and read and read and read.

ETHAN. That sounds great.

OLIVIA. It was.

ETHAN. So?

OLIVIA. He, uh, he just ended up not being who I thought he was.

ETHAN. Too bad. Most girls I know would kill for a situation like that. All in exchange for sleeping with some Italian guy —

OLIVIA. It wasn't an *exchange*, it was a relationship.

ETHAN. And then what?

OLIVIA. What? My other relationships?

ETHAN. Yes.

OLIVIA. Um, I don't know. A couple great guys. A couple not-so-great guys.

ETHAN. What happened to the good ones?

OLIVIA. The usual ... got a job in a different city, doesn't want to be serious, wants to be too serious ... but isn't it always a little ... *who knows* and how does this *ever* work.

ETHAN. It is. So, are you with anyone now?

OLIVIA. *(Surprised by the question.)* Uh, no. Are you?

ETHAN. Nope. So, you speak Italian?

OLIVIA. *Si, si ... se vuoi, posso parlare italiano la prossima volta che scopiamo.*

ETHAN. *(No idea what she said.)* Cool. *(They kiss.)* So, where's your new book?

OLIVIA. In my room. Why?

ETHAN. I want to read it now.

OLIVIA. Well, you can't.

ETHAN. Come on!

OLIVIA. No.

ETHAN. We did what we did last night but you won't let me read your book?

OLIVIA. Nope.

ETHAN. Why not?

OLIVIA. Too personal.

ETHAN. Come on! I'm sure I'll love it.

OLIVIA. That's not the point.

ETHAN. Right. The point is you like it and everyone else can fuck off.

OLIVIA. No. The point is, if you read it, I'll want you to like it and I don't want to want you to like it. I want to not care. But I will. This is my problem. And, for years, I've worked really hard and spent a lot of money on ... *(Finding the right words.)* health-care professionals trying to stop wanting people to like what I'm doing. To just do it.

ETHAN. That's good.

OLIVIA. But, I can't. I'm sure if my first book had done better, I'd feel differently. But knowing my work is good and never having had that response? I still care.

ETHAN. Well, it's not like you can totally not care. I mean, everybody cares a little.

OLIVIA. Yeah. But it felt so important to me to be … *important*, you know?

ETHAN. Whatever that means.

OLIVIA. To make something that people would think was … brilliant.

ETHAN. But a lot of people will!

OLIVIA. Now, I just want to be happy. And people misunderstanding or dismissing my work made me really unhappy. So, I'm not showing it to anyone right now. I'm just writing what I want. No compromises. No second guessing. No hopes. No expectations.

ETHAN. But you have to have some expectations or you wouldn't be writing.

OLIVIA. *(Joking.)* Sure. Maybe it'll be discovered after I'm dead and everyone will think it's a masterpiece and feel sorry for me that I wasn't celebrated in my own time.

ETHAN. Who are you, Emily Dickinson?!

OLIVIA. *(Re: the Dickinson reference.)* Good one.

ETHAN. Well, she got mixed reviews, too. And so do I. But, we're proof that you shouldn't be discouraged by the assholes' response.

OLIVIA. It's not just that.

ETHAN. What then?

OLIVIA. If something was going to happen for me, it would have already.

ETHAN. Now, that's crazy.

OLIVIA. Why? People I know from school are on their third or fourth book. Some have been successful so long they're on the *comeback* phase of their career. They're making a comeback and I never got anywhere.

ETHAN. Because you stopped trying!

OLIVIA. I mean, Ahmit, who, when I met him at twenty, had only written short stories. *I* convinced him to try writing a novel. He has a *Pulitzer*.

ETHAN. But that doesn't mean that you aren't as good as he is.

OLIVIA. I know. Maybe. But there comes a time when you have to face that no matter how good you think you are, things are probably not going to work out the way you wanted.

ETHAN. But you can't give up when you have something new to // put out —

OLIVIA. Look, I don't want to compete with the twenty-two-year-olds trying to get off square one, trying to have my little voice heard over the throngs of hundreds and millions. At this point, it would be stupid.

ETHAN. You don't have to think of it as competing against anyone.

OLIVIA. And isn't the world already choking on all the shallow, trivial observations of millions of self-important morons? Not you.

ETHAN. Thanks.

OLIVIA. So, why should I try to fight my way through that?

ETHAN. Because unlike most of the shit that's out there, your writing is incredibly good.

OLIVIA. But what if people don't respond to this new one that I think is my best yet? What do I do then?

ETHAN. If it's even *half* as good as the one I read, it is a huge loss to the world if people can't read it.

OLIVIA. Why are you being so nice to me?

ETHAN. Why are you being so suspect?

OLIVIA. I just keep waiting for the asshole to show up.

ETHAN. Well, he'll be here tomorrow. So, if there's anything you want to do with the nice guy, we've got some time. *(Ethan moves to her and kisses her. Passionately. It escalates. Clothes come off. Sex is imminent.)*

Scene 3

The next day. Late afternoon. Ethan sits in the living room, a few pages into reading The Lover *by Marguerite Duras.*

Olivia enters from the bedroom.

OLIVIA. *(Sleepy.)* There you are.

ETHAN. Sorry. I never got to sleep.

OLIVIA. Ugh … what time is it?

ETHAN. Around four-thirty, I think.

OLIVIA. In the afternoon? Oh my God. You're kidding.

ETHAN. *(Smiling.)* I'm not. We didn't go to bed until five or something.

OLIVIA. Still. I can't believe I'm getting up at four-thirty in the afternoon.

ETHAN. You want something? Coffee? Beer?

OLIVIA. Coffee. Thanks. *(Ethan goes to the kitchen to get it. Calling to him.)* You get some work done on your screenplay?

ETHAN. No. The notes from the studio are too stupid to face.

OLIVIA. So, what have you been doing?

ETHAN. Reading.

OLIVIA. You're going to miss your deadline.

ETHAN. It's the least of my worries, really. I should also be working on this app I'm developing.

OLIVIA. You do that, too?

ETHAN. Not the technical side. Just the idea and the content. Here. *(He hands Olivia the coffee.)*

OLIVIA. Thanks. So, what is it?

ETHAN. You know "Band of the Day"?

OLIVIA. Not literally but I get what you mean.

ETHAN. It's like that, the literary form of Band of the Day — Writer of the Day basically. It's impossible to slog through everything now, hard for undiscovered writers to get above the noise. So, my app will introduce people to hand-picked, very cool new writers and selections of their stuff, which you'll be able to buy and download with a click. And based on what you say you like, you'll get personalized recommendations; if you like that guy, you'll like this guy.

OLIVIA. Like the Pandora thumbs up?

ETHAN. Basically, yeah.

OLIVIA. That sounds really good, actually.

ETHAN. Thanks so much, actually. I'm also getting some exclusive releases of shorter pieces by better-known writers. That'll help attract people to the site.

OLIVIA. And you'll make money from the downloads?

ETHAN. Yeah. I'm going to take less of a cut than other places do, though. Works out for everyone. But I'm not in it for the money.

OLIVIA. No?

ETHAN. I want it to be really respected and, eventually, once it's established, and people are thinking of me in this new way …

OLIVIA. You'll put out your novel?

ETHAN. Right. But instead of doing any of that. I read all day. *(Holding up* The Lover.*)* This *is* really good.

OLIVIA. I told you.

ETHAN. I think you write like her.

OLIVIA. Like Marguerite Duras?

ETHAN. Not like her, exactly, but the effect. It's spare but really evocative. And kind-of sharp, like … a little brutal. Honest. Confident. I like it.

OLIVIA. I'm glad.

ETHAN. But there's something I just finished that I think is better.

OLIVIA. *(Doubtful.)* Really? What? *(Ethan pulls out Olivia's manuscript.)*

ETHAN. This.

OLIVIA. *(In shock, unable to process.)* What…?

ETHAN. It's totally incredible.

OLIVIA. Why … why would you do that?

ETHAN. I think it's brilliant.

OLIVIA. *(Slowly, not really hearing him.)* I can't believe you did that.

ETHAN. You need to get over yourself, Olivia. People need to read this.

OLIVIA. I think … I think you should go.

ETHAN. What?

OLIVIA. *(Reaching for the manuscript.)* You need to go.

ETHAN. *(Keeping the manuscript away from her.)* No. No. No. You do not get to write something like this and keep it to yourself.

OLIVIA. *(Very forcefully.)* Give it to me!

ETHAN. Olivia …

OLIVIA. *(Almost violently.)* Give it to me!

ETHAN. *(Giving the manuscript to her.)* OK.

OLIVIA. You had no right.

ETHAN. I wanted to read it // so I could —

OLIVIA. I don't care what you wanted!

ETHAN. Did you hear me? I think it's totally brilliant!

OLIVIA. And, what? That's supposed to make me grateful that you stole my book and read it without my permission?

ETHAN. Look. You told me you wanted someone to discover it and think it's incredible. That wasn't you basically telling me // to read it and — ?

OLIVIA. If I wanted you to read it, I would have given it to you.

ETHAN. Listen to me. I think it's fucking incredible. You can't keep this from the world.

OLIVIA. I *can't*? Look, you don't know me. You don't know me *at all*.

ETHAN. That's not totally true.

OLIVIA. If you knew me, you wouldn't have done this. You would have waited until I was ready // to give it to you —

ETHAN. No, clearly, you need someone to push you.

OLIVIA. Your arrogance really knows no limits.

ETHAN. Look. I'm sorry if you're mad I read it. But I can't be. No. I won't be. And it's a fucking tragedy if no one else does. This book is everything. It's funny, it's moving, it's subtle. And surprising. Her inner life is, like, blindingly vivid. Best of all, it's really, really honest. It's remarkable. *(After a moment.)* So. I'm not sorry Olivia. I'm not. *(After a moment.)* OK?

OLIVIA. *(Slowly, reluctantly persuaded by him.)* Uh … OK.

ETHAN. You want a glass of water or something?

OLIVIA. No. I'm all right.

ETHAN. *(After a beat.)* Listen, I get you not wanting to be exposed or whatever. But to keep this book to yourself? It's too good. So, what if no one knew it was you? Self-publish under a made-up name, a made-up profile, and put out the book that way.

OLIVIA. You mean lie?

ETHAN. It doesn't matter. It's the internet.

OLIVIA. Right. But …

ETHAN. Come on, Olivia! It'd be so good for you to see what people have to say about the writer you are now, get you not so cut off from the world.

OLIVIA. I'm not cut off from the world.

ETHAN. Look, you can just put it out there and see what happens. I could set it up in, like, ten minutes, walk you through all of it. You just have to be a little brave.

OLIVIA. No.

ETHAN. Why?

OLIVIA. I don't want to open that door again.

ETHAN. But … what? You had twenty reviews of your first book?

OLIVIA. More like eight or so.

ETHAN. Now you can have eight hundred of the new one!

OLIVIA. Those aren't reviews.

ETHAN. Not like from a newspaper, but —

OLIVIA. Right. I don't want to subject myself to a bunch of anonymous strangers saying horrible, misspelled things about my work. I don't know how you deal with that.

ETHAN. Well, I'm an egomaniac. I don't care what they say as long as they say something. And I know that being popular isn't the same as being good. But at least be part of the conversation. Come on. *No one will know it's you!*

OLIVIA. What they say will still be about my work.

ETHAN. And it's incredible! People are going to love it. Not everyone, of course, but —

OLIVIA. This is what I'm saying. No matter how good it is there will be cruel idiots who will feel the need to trash it and I don't want to have to subject myself // to —

ETHAN. But they don't matter. Take what's good and leave the rest behind.

OLIVIA. That doesn't make sense. You have to take all of it or none of it, it seems to me. And how do I make myself hard enough to withstand all the bad but stay soft enough to still be the writer I want to be? It seems impossible.

ETHAN. Look — I'm giving you another chance to show the world how talented you are. Take it. It's worth the risk.

OLIVIA. I just can't.

ETHAN. Come on, Olivia.

OLIVIA. *(With total finality.)* Ethan.

ETHAN. OK. OK. But I think it's remarkable. I do. And I'm honored to have read it. No matter how mad you are at me.

OLIVIA. *(Very slowly.)* Well … Thank you. For all you said about it. Really.

ETHAN. *(After a moment.)* What about your first book, then? The one that was so misunderstood? Let me at least post that one this way. Did the rights revert back to you yet?

OLIVIA. Yes. But …

ETHAN. Perfect. We'll change the title, make a new cover that doesn't totally suck, make it seem like it's new. We'll post it with the fake name, fake bio. I'll get it some attention and you can see what more people think of it.

OLIVIA. I don't know.

ETHAN. It's so easy. You don't have to wait for anybody's permission anymore.

OLIVIA. That's why every crackpot hack is doing it.

ETHAN. Let's just upload the book and see what happens.

OLIVIA. I *have* thought about this. I've even looked at KDP and Smashwords. A couple others. But the magnitude of … crap. The whole thing just feels … desperate.

ETHAN. It's the way it is now.

OLIVIA. I know. But …

ETHAN. You think your chance is over, now you can see that it's not. You can have the life for that book that you always wanted.

OLIVIA. Why are you offering to do all of this?

ETHAN. Because I can. Because I want to. But, mostly, because you're sitting here in obscurity and it's bullshit. It's wrong. You deserve so much more than what you have. We both know you do.

OLIVIA. I don't know that anyone *deserves* anything.

ETHAN. Do you love teaching?

OLIVIA. Uh … yeah. Yeah, I do.

ETHAN. You love your job?

OLIVIA. I really like my job. Yeah.

ETHAN. You teach where you want to teach?

OLIVIA. I like my students a lot.

ETHAN. So, everything's how you want it to be?

OLIVIA. Jesus, you're young. When is *everything* how you want it to be?

ETHAN. So, you're not happy where you are?

OLIVIA. I am. But, come on, most of the really great jobs go to people who have had more success than I have.

ETHAN. So, it would be helpful — more success? There'd be something to gain if your first book had a second life?

OLIVIA. Sure. Hypothetically. Yes.

ETHAN. So, we'll put it out there again — all pseudonym-ed and protected — and we'll see what happens, OK?

OLIVIA. *(Still struggling.)* Oh, man …

ETHAN. Come on.

OLIVIA. *(Getting there.)* Aaaggghhh …

ETHAN. Come on! You know you want to!

OLIVIA. OK!

ETHAN. OK! Let's do this! I'll set it up right now.

OLIVIA. Not right now.

ETHAN. Yes, *right now. (Ethan goes to his computer and clicks around.)* If I give you any more time, you'll change your mind.

OLIVIA. Ethan …

ETHAN. First thing we need to think of is your name. What do you think of … "Cat"?

OLIVIA. *(With disdain.)* What?

ETHAN. Cat. It's, like, short for Catherine.

OLIVIA. Cat?

ETHAN. What's wrong with Cat?

OLIVIA. Absolutely not.

ETHAN. So what do you say?

OLIVIA. I'm not doing this right now.

ETHAN. *(Typing.)* Then your name is Cat.

OLIVIA. No! Stop!

ETHAN. So…? What?

OLIVIA. I don't know. Lily?

ETHAN. Nope.

OLIVIA. Maggie?

ETHAN. Really?

OLIVIA. Emma?

ETHAN. I like Emma. *(Typing.)* OK! Last name?

OLIVIA. Joe?

ETHAN. *(With exaggerated country twang.)* Emma Joe?

OLIVIA. OK. Well, it should be something short, strong …

ETHAN. Raines? Reese? Ren? Hen? No. Hall? Lane? Hall is close.

OLIVIA. Thorne?

ETHAN. A little too Gothic maybe.

OLIVIA. Emma Lunt?

ETHAN. No. You're gonna want to avoid that, believe me.

OLIVIA. Emma Thorn could work — without an "e."

ETHAN. Yeah …

OLIVIA. It's smart-sounding to me. Classic.

ETHAN. Emma Thorn. OK. Yeah. Yeah, it's good.

OLIVIA. Wait — what about just initials? E. M.? No.

ETHAN. So they don't know if you're a guy or a girl? You think that'll help somehow?

OLIVIA. *(Sarcastic.)* Well, being a woman is always such a huge advantage as an artist and I'd like to see how I do without that leg up.

ETHAN. OK. Sure. *(Realizing.)* You're kidding. But cool. Like J. K. Rowling. I like it.

OLIVIA. *(Typing.)* E. S.? E. S. Thorn?

ETHAN. E. S. Thorn. OK. How about twenty-nine?

OLIVIA. For what?

ETHAN. Your age. Not too young, not too old.

OLIVIA. Whatever.

ETHAN. OK. Other profile stuff.

OLIVIA. Meaning what?

ETHAN. You know, things that define you. Basically, like, one sentence that totally encapsulates who you are.

OLIVIA. *(With deep scorn.)* One sentence that totally encapsulates who I am?

ETHAN. Nevermind. OK. As soon as I'm back online, I'll upload the book to Amazon, tweet the link to get some more traffic —

OLIVIA. I don't think your followers would be // interested in my —

ETHAN. What? Too good for my people? I have half a million followers.

OLIVIA. That's insane.

ETHAN. And my readers are smarter than you think. And seriously loyal. If I say "check this out," they will. Even some of the fucking highbrow crowd condescend to follow me. Do you have a copy of it on your computer?

OLIVIA. Yes.

ETHAN. *(Teasing her.)* Is it in Word '97?

OLIVIA. Shut up. *(After a second.)* I think it is, actually.

ETHAN. It's fine. I can convert it.

OLIVIA. Here. *(Olivia hands him her large, bulky, outdated computer. He sets it down and gets a flash drive out of his bag.)*

ETHAN. So you know, once the book's up, I will have to add some fake comments.

OLIVIA. Fake comments?

ETHAN. To make it look like some people have read it.

OLIVIA. That feels like cheating.

ETHAN. Everybody does it.

OLIVIA. The best justification ever.

ETHAN. They'll mostly be good. But I'll have to write a couple mean ones, just to be realistic.

OLIVIA. Well, make sure the spelling is really bad on those.

ETHAN. I will.

OLIVIA. This whole thing is making me // a little —

ETHAN. It's going to be great.

OLIVIA. And no one will know?

ETHAN. No one. I promise. Just me.

OLIVIA. All right. You're very persuasive.

ETHAN. And I'll admit, it'll be good for me, too. When my app launches, I'll have already discovered the incredible E. S. Thorn. I'll be brilliant by association. *(Re: trying to find the book on her computer.)* It's under…?

OLIVIA. The folder very secretively named "books" on the desktop.

ETHAN. Got it. *(Ethan plugs in the flash drive, clicks around.)*

OLIVIA. How have you done all of this? Your big career. I mean, it's incredibly impressive. When I was twenty-five, I didn't know my ass from my elbow.

ETHAN. Well, I'm twenty-eight now.

OLIVIA. Right. In that case, I'm not impressed.

ETHAN. *(Gesturing to her open computer.)* You wrote this incredible book around twenty-five, right?

OLIVIA. Yes, but you … you seem so fully formed.

ETHAN. You do, too.

OLIVIA. Yeah, well, it'd be a little sad if I didn't by this point.

ETHAN. It's just most of the girls I meet … they're all so … not.

OLIVIA. Maybe it's just the messy ones are drawn to you.

ETHAN. Maybe.

OLIVIA. I was a confused mess then.

ETHAN. I bet people that knew you then wouldn't say that.

OLIVIA. I think they might.

ETHAN. Anyway, you turned out pretty well, and that's what matters, right? And a lot of people would say I'm a mess now.

OLIVIA. No you're not. I mean, what do you even worry about?

ETHAN. What do you mean?

OLIVIA. People worry about money, being successful, being lonely, right?

ETHAN. *(Among other things.)* Yeah …

OLIVIA. And you seem to have all of that covered. So, what do you worry about?

ETHAN. Sure, but what I have isn't all I want.

OLIVIA. *(Encouraging him to say more.)* No?

ETHAN. No. I do think my novel has the potential to be … significant.

OLIVIA. You do?

ETHAN. I do.

OLIVIA. Well, should I read *Sex with Strangers* in the meantime?

ETHAN. *(Strongly.)* No, don't. I don't want you to. No.

OLIVIA. Why not?

ETHAN. I don't want that stuff to be the first thing of mine that you read. *(A second of vulnerability.)* I'm … I'm glad for what they've done for me. But until I prove that I'm not just that guy from those books, until I write what I want to write … and prove that I deserve to be — *(Strongly shifting gears, overly confident.)* You know, people think they know me. What I can do. What I can't. But they're wrong.

33

OLIVIA. OK.

ETHAN. And I don't want the *Sex with Strangers* stuff in your head. What I want to do is so different. So, don't read it, OK?

OLIVIA. OK.

ETHAN. *(Strongly.)* Promise me.

OLIVIA. *(After a moment.)* OK. *(Ethan removes the flash drive and puts it in his bag.)*

ETHAN. *(After a moment, a shift of energy.)* Hey — is there someplace to eat around here?

OLIVIA. What? Like a restaurant?

ETHAN. Yeah.

OLIVIA. Near the lake. Not too far.

ETHAN. Let's go out tonight.

OLIVIA. What, like, out to dinner or something?

ETHAN. Yeah.

OLIVIA. Like on a date out to dinner?

ETHAN. Yeah. Like on a date.

OLIVIA. No.

ETHAN. Why not?

OLIVIA. I don't want to go out on a date with you. Ten minutes ago I was kicking you out.

ETHAN. And, yet, I'm still here.

OLIVIA. Yeah, why is that?

ETHAN. Because you are so into me.

OLIVIA. Oh my God! I am not. You're a dick and a liar and a thief!

ETHAN. And you couldn't be more into me. *(They kiss.)* Come on, let's go out. It's my last night.

OLIVIA. It is?

ETHAN. Yeah. I have to head back to Chicago in the morning. I fly out to LA tomorrow night.

OLIVIA. Oh. I … I didn't know.

ETHAN. I don't want to go, believe me.

OLIVIA. Yeah …

ETHAN. When I get back from LA, we should go to Paris.

OLIVIA. What?

ETHAN. I've never been. Haven't traveled much, actually.

OLIVIA. Well, Paris is … beautiful.

ETHAN. So, we should go.

OLIVIA. But we're not — I mean — do you want to see me?

ETHAN. Yes, I do.

OLIVIA. No, I mean, actually see me.

ETHAN. Yeah.

OLIVIA. I mean me — not me and a bunch of other people.

ETHAN. Yeah. I want to see you. And my hunch is if I want to see you, I only see you.

OLIVIA. Yeah.

ETHAN. So, I'll just see you.

OLIVIA. But, we're not, I mean, it's not like we're going to have a real relationship, right?

ETHAN. Why not?

OLIVIA. Because I'm probably too old for you.

ETHAN. You might think you're too old for me, but I don't.

OLIVIA. It's only because you're too young to know I'm too old.

ETHAN. Mr. Italiano wasn't too old for you.

OLIVIA. And that ended badly.

ETHAN. Because he was a dick.

OLIVIA. *(Teasing him.)* I thought you were a dick.

ETHAN. Right. But really.

OLIVIA. You're serious?

ETHAN. I am. Aren't you?

OLIVIA. *(After a moment.)* I could be.

ETHAN. OK. Good.

OLIVIA. I'll just put it out of my head that in ten years you'll still be perfect, and I'll be … *(Calculates for a second.) Jesus!* I'll be …

ETHAN. Ten years?! Can we just think about right now?

OLIVIA. Yeah. Yeah, we can. *(They kiss. Clothes come off. Sex is imminent.)*

Scene 4

Olivia and Ethan appear in the bedroom doorway, kissing. Ethan breaks away.

ETHAN. I'm so late! *(They kiss again. Ethan breaks away.)* I'm so, so late! *(They kiss again. Ethan breaks away.)* I'm going to be really busy but I'll call you when I can.

OLIVIA. OK.

ETHAN. I'll — do you see my other boot?

OLIVIA. *(After looking around.)* Here it is.

ETHAN. I'll be back in a week.

OLIVIA. A *week*?!

ETHAN. I know. *(Looking at his phone.)* Hey — I think the wireless is back up.

OLIVIA. Really? That must have been who was at the door. We should have gotten it.

ETHAN. He must've fixed what he needed to outside, 'cause I'm on. See if you can get on.

OLIVIA. OK. *(Olivia opens her computer and clicks around.)*

ETHAN. So, no wifi password here, huh?

OLIVIA. Nope.

ETHAN. That is quaint. Are you on?

OLIVIA. Almost …

ETHAN. *(Looking at his phone.)* I have email! Oh, fuck me.

OLIVIA. What?

ETHAN. I have eight hundred and thirty-nine emails in my inbox.

OLIVIA. I have … *(Looking at her screen as her email loads.)* seven.

ETHAN. And there's a Twitter feed about me being dead.

OLIVIA. No.

ETHAN. I told you. *(Speaking as he types.)* Hey Motherfuckers! Sorry to disappoint you!

OLIVIA. *(Getting his attention.)* Hey. *(Ethan goes to her. They kiss.)*

ETHAN. I took a couple of your books.

OLIVIA. Oh?

ETHAN. I'm holding them hostage. That way no matter how much you freak out, you still have to see me again.

OLIVIA. I'm not going to freak out. Why would I freak out? Why do you think I'm going to freak out?

ETHAN. Wild guess. *(They kiss.)* And I'm going to set up a meeting for you with my agent.

OLIVIA. What? No.

ETHAN. Yeah.

OLIVIA. I couldn't ask you to do that.

ETHAN. You're not asking. I'm offering. It's not a big deal.

OLIVIA. It is.

ETHAN. It's not. I make them a lot of money, so she meets who I ask her to.

OLIVIA. Well …

ETHAN. It's so easy. And I want to.

OLIVIA. OK. Well. That would be great. Thank you. *(They kiss.)*

ETHAN. Sorry. I have to go.

OLIVIA. I know.

ETHAN. Bye.

OLIVIA. Bye. *(Ethan leaves. Olivia watches his car drive off. She sits on the couch and opens a book. She looks to her computer. She looks to her book. She looks to the computer. She puts down the book and pulls the computer towards her. Typing.)* "Ethan Strange. *Sex with Strangers.*" *(She hesitates, then hits a button to search. She clicks on something and begins to read. Horrified, slowly.)* Oh … my … God … *(Lights.)*

End of Act One

ACT TWO

Scene 5

One week later. Olivia's apartment. Evening. The sounds of the city. There are many, many books on shelves and in stacks all over the room. Ethan, holding a small suitcase, and Olivia kiss. After a moment, they break apart.

ETHAN. That was a long week.

OLIVIA. Are you hungry?

ETHAN. No. I'm good. *(Ethan sets down his bag, kisses Olivia and pulls her to the sofa. She breaks away.)*

OLIVIA. So, it seems like it went well.

ETHAN. Yeah, it did. Sorry we didn't talk more but things were crazy.

OLIVIA. No. You were in touch a lot considering how busy you were. *(Ethan moves in to kiss her.)* Can we talk for a second? You just walked in the door.

ETHAN. Yeah. Sure. *(A text chime from Ethan's phone. During the next exchange, he reads and texts throughout.)*

OLIVIA. So, your meetings were good?

ETHAN. Yeah, really good. It was insane, though, work all day, and then my manager kept taking me out to all those fucking parties ...

OLIVIA. They weren't fun?

ETHAN. It was fine for a couple days, but I'd lose my mind, I think, if I actually *lived* there. Anyway, they treated me like a rock star, so who am I to complain about it?

OLIVIA. That's great.

ETHAN. No. The great part is, I just heard from Junot Díaz and he's going to give me an exclusive release of a new short story.

OLIVIA. For your app?

ETHAN. Yes!

OLIVIA. *(Genuinely impressed.)* Whoa. That's amazing.

ETHAN. It is. *(Ethan finally pulls himself away from the phone and looks around the room, seeing all the books.)* Wow. This place is a frigging library.

OLIVIA. I know. It borders on a sickness.

ETHAN. I have your books I took. *(Ethan takes them out of his bag and gives them to Olivia.)*

OLIVIA. Thanks.

ETHAN. I read them both.

OLIVIA. You did? Did you like them?

ETHAN. I did. The Tolstoy short stories the most.

OLIVIA. These P&V translations are great. You ever read him before?

ETHAN. I started *War and Peace* once.

OLIVIA. You started with *War and Peace*?

ETHAN. I didn't say finish it. I've read Dostoyevsky. Gogol. But no Tolstoy.

OLIVIA. Until now.

ETHAN. I'm catching up. *(As he leans in to kiss her, a text chime from his phone. Olivia pulls back. Re: reading the text.)* Oh, man.

OLIVIA. What?

ETHAN. It's nothing. My mom.

OLIVIA. She OK?

ETHAN. Yeah. It's, uh, it's her birthday next month and she's been sending me these texts with pictures of some "suggestions."

OLIVIA. Is that sweet or weird?

ETHAN. I don't know. But I think I was happier when she wouldn't accept my gifts because she was so mortified by me, her son, the asshole public-sex maniac. At least then it seemed like she expected more of me. Now, it's like she believes this is the best I'll ever do so she might as well enjoy it! I mean, she, of all people on earth, she knows me, and yet, the bigger things get, the more she gives up on me …

OLIVIA. I'm sorry.

ETHAN. *(Shaking it off.)* It's fine. *(Remembering.)* Hey, I got you something.

OLIVIA. What do you mean? Like a present?

ETHAN. Yes.

OLIVIA. Why?

ETHAN. Because I wanted to. What? Don't you like presents?

OLIVIA. No. I love presents.

ETHAN. All right then. *(Ethan pulls out an iPad Mini from his bag and presents it to her.)*

OLIVIA. *(Unsure.)* Oh.

ETHAN. *(Joking.)* It's called an iPad.

OLIVIA. Shut up.

ETHAN. We can put all your books on it so you won't have to carry them around anymore.

OLIVIA. *(Not impressed.)* Huh.

ETHAN. I got you the small one 'cause it's more like holding a book. *(Tapping the iPad.)* I already loaded a couple of your favorites.

OLIVIA. You did?

ETHAN. Yeah.

OLIVIA. That was really thoughtful.

ETHAN. You like it?

OLIVIA. *(Smells the iPad.)* Smells like the future.

ETHAN. *(Re: the iPad.)* And with this, you can also check your book sales whenever, wherever. Here. *(He taps something on the iPad.)* See.

OLIVIA. Great.

ETHAN. It's exciting, isn't it!

OLIVIA. *(Vaguely.)* Yeah …

ETHAN. You haven't checked your sales, have you? Have you even seen the page for your book?

OLIVIA. No.

ETHAN. Olivia!

OLIVIA. I'm too scared. Being out there again … I know that might be hard for you to understand, but …

ETHAN. Olivia! E. S. Thorn sold three hundred books.

OLIVIA. What?!

ETHAN. In a week. At $2.99, it's not a lot of money yet, but for someone unknown that's actually really good. It's gaining momentum and the comments are — OK, we're looking at them right now.

OLIVIA. No.

ETHAN. *(Pulling it up on the iPad.)* Come on.

OLIVIA. I can't.

ETHAN. You can.

OLIVIA. No. I feel like I'm about to throw up.

ETHAN. So, what? You want me to read them to you?

OLIVIA. *(Full of anxiety.)* No. I don't! // Really!

ETHAN. OK. Some are about the excerpts, some the whole book.

OLIVIA. I don't want to hear them! // Really, Ethan! Don't!

ETHAN. OK. There are fifty-seven comments.

OLIVIA. Fifty-seven?!

ETHAN. *(Reading comment.)* "I love your writing! It's smart, bold, aching, and funny."

OLIVIA. Really?

ETHAN. *(Reading.)* "Beyond the humor (which is great) the intense moments of sadness give this real soul."

OLIVIA. That's really nice.

ETHAN. "This made me LAUGH" — laugh in all caps. "Buying the book now!!!!!!" — six exclamation points.

OLIVIA. That's a lot of punctuation.

ETHAN. This is a good one — "Where's a profile pic? I bet you're as hot as your writing."

OLIVIA. Oh, God. *(A tiny beat.)* OK. What about the bad ones?

ETHAN. There aren't that many.

OLIVIA. OK. Go on.

ETHAN. Are you ready?

OLIVIA. No. *(Gathering herself.)* OK. Go.

ETHAN. "Boring."

OLIVIA. Is that all?

ETHAN. *(Reading the full entry.)* "This was boring to me."

OLIVIA. OK.

ETHAN. *(Reading a different entry, with increasing rage.)* "I am older than your average reader, I imagine, but I found your writing shocking, crass, and not the kind of thing I think most Americans enjoy."

OLIVIA. Seriously? *I'm* crass?

ETHAN. See, you're putting it all in perspective.

OLIVIA. Is he calling my writing un-American?

ETHAN. I think he is.

OLIVIA. *(Takes the iPad and looks at the comments.)* Kook.

ETHAN. Yup.

OLIVIA. *(In response to seeing something, as though wounded.)* Ohhhhhh. *(Reading a comment.)* "Remarkably self-indulgent and completely trivial."

ETHAN. How do you feel?

OLIVIA. Bad.

ETHAN. *Really* bad?

OLIVIA. No. Just a little bad. But I'll feel worse, if I keep going. "Empty narcissism."

ETHAN. I wrote that one.

OLIVIA. You did?

ETHAN. Yeah, that is a fake one.

OLIVIA. I love how you spelled it "narcis-sis-sis-ism." Thank you.

ETHAN. Sure.

OLIVIA. Wait. Did you write all the positive ones?

ETHAN. Only one.

OLIVIA. Which one.

ETHAN. I'm not telling.

OLIVIA. The nicest one?

ETHAN. No, actually.

OLIVIA. Did you write the hot one?

ETHAN. The "are you as hot as your writing" one?

OLIVIA. Yes.

ETHAN. Yes.

OLIVIA. Cute. *(Looking at the screen.)* OK. That's just mean. And disgusting. "Your writing sucks a filthy whore's twat."

ETHAN. Ignore it. I'll delete it later for "inappropriate content." And Jonathan Lethem retweeted the link.

OLIVIA. What? Jonathan Lethem?!

ETHAN. Yeah.

OLIVIA. No! You're kidding!

ETHAN. I'm not. I'll show you. *(Tapping the iPad.)* And, you know, Susan, my agent, she loved it, too.

OLIVIA. She did? What did she say?

ETHAN. Thought it was fucking great. I told her the new one was even better and she wants to read it. She didn't call you?

OLIVIA. No, she didn't.

ETHAN. She will. *(Pointing to the screen.)* See. Jonathan Lethem recommends ...

OLIVIA. *(Looking at the screen.)* Holy shit! Holy. Fucking. Shit!

ETHAN. See, it's not so bad, huh?

OLIVIA. I can't even.

ETHAN. You did it. I'm proud of you.

OLIVIA. What? You did it.

ETHAN. *(Cockily.)* OK. Yeah. I did.

OLIVIA. Thank you.

ETHAN. OK. Was that enough talking? *(Ethan gently takes the iPad away from Olivia and moves in on her. They kiss. It escalates. Clothes start coming off. Olivia breaks away.)*

OLIVIA. I can't. I —

ETHAN. *(Shocked, confused.)* What? What is it?

OLIVIA. *(After a long, bad silence.)* I, uh …

ETHAN. What is it?

OLIVIA. While you were in LA, I, uh …

ETHAN. Yeah…?

OLIVIA. I read your book.

ETHAN. Oh.

OLIVIA. The first one. That was all I could handle.

ETHAN. I asked you not to read it.

OLIVIA. I know. I'm sorry. I wasn't going to. But I googled you and … there was so much. I started reading all of that and I couldn't stop and I read the book. I see why you didn't want me to.

ETHAN. 'Cause you hate me now?

OLIVIA. Well, it wasn't fun, reading about you having sex with a hundred other women. And … *(Difficult for her to say.)* all the webcam stuff and the underground sex parties — all of that — I find really creepy. I mean, I'm not like that. I'm not interested in that …

ETHAN. That's fine. I've already done all that shit.

OLIVIA. That's not the point. The thing that really bothered me was the way you talk about those girls. I mean, who is that guy? You walk in here and I don't see him at all.

ETHAN. He's not me. Not anymore.

OLIVIA. The picture on the book jacket is you.

ETHAN. What I wrote about … I did that stuff years ago.

OLIVIA. Like five.

ETHAN. That's a long time.

OLIVIA. Is it?

ETHAN. And, anyway, I told you, a lot of things are, you know, embellished.

OLIVIA. Like what?

ETHAN. Like the really bad stuff.

OLIVIA. Isn't that most of it?

ETHAN. I wouldn't say *most* of it but … come on. You know me well enough to know that I wouldn't // do a lot of that —

OLIVIA. Do I?

ETHAN. Don't say that. Why didn't you tell me about this right away?

OLIVIA. I wanted to see you. I didn't want to talk about it on the phone. I mean … I also found a bunch of those sites … women that wrote about you. Wrote about being with you.

ETHAN. OK, you have to know, most of that is bullshit.

OLIVIA. They make you sound like such a — I don't even know what the word would be. All the ones I can think of are too charming. But you sounded … dangerous.

ETHAN. Show me what you're talking about.

OLIVIA. *(Getting her computer.)* Uh … OK.

ETHAN. Look, ever since word got out about the movie happening, people are coming out of the woodwork, saying shit, most of whom I've never met. You can't take them at // face-value —

OLIVIA. A lot of them had really personal information about you. *(Hard for her to say.)* Including one who wrote an incredibly graphic description of what you do, of your face, when you're about to …

ETHAN. A bunch of them probably have slept with me, OK? So, yeah, they've got that information. But everything else? You can't believe it.

OLIVIA. Here's one.

ETHAN. *(Looking at the screen.)* Oh, God. Come on! She — this girl, Whitney, she, I dated her when I was *nineteen*! I mean, fuck! Am I going to be held accountable for every stupid thing — I mean, can you defend everything you did at nineteen?

OLIVIA. Well, the record of everything I did before the age of twenty-one is in one large cardboard box at the bottom of my closet, so I'm not really the one to ask.

ETHAN. You never broke someone's heart or did something you're not exactly proud of — ?

OLIVIA. Of course. Of course. But you humiliated these women in such an awful way.

ETHAN. I did some stupid shit. OK? I'm not saying I didn't. But all of the girls I wrote about knew — *because I told them* — that I was going to be a total asshole.

OLIVIA. And that makes it OK?

ETHAN. Every one of them was OK with it.

OLIVIA. I can't believe that's true. You left drunk girls naked and unconscious in pools of their own vomit, never knowing if they ever got home // all right —

ETHAN. I'm not saying I'm proud of it. All right? // But —

OLIVIA. You left that girl in the middle of the highway.

ETHAN. *That* never happened. I fucking made that up.

OLIVIA. And you think that's OK? That you made up even more shocking, more *horrifying* things, and let people think you not only did them, but that it was something to brag about, to imitate?

ETHAN. That's not me. That's Ethan Strange.

OLIVIA. I don't understand the difference.

ETHAN. Look, how have I been to *you*. Not to those girls. To *you?*

OLIVIA. Amazing.

ETHAN. So, can we just focus on what's in the room? Please?

OLIVIA. I want to. I do.

ETHAN. Look, I want to be with you. And I thought maybe you felt the same way.

OLIVIA. I did. But the things that are in my head now …

ETHAN. Why are you letting some shit from the past that may or may not even be true // keep you from —

OLIVIA. Those girls, so many of them, seemed so funny and smart and more beautiful than I ever was, and you were *merciless* about them. To them. That that *judgment* could be directed at me —

ETHAN. It won't be.

OLIVIA. That one day you might treat me // like that —

ETHAN. I wouldn't.

OLIVIA. It makes me … afraid of you.

ETHAN. I told you I won't write about you. I promised you I won't.

OLIVIA. Yeah // but —

ETHAN. And for the rest? You have to trust me.

OLIVIA. How do I do that?

ETHAN. It's in the past. I'm different now. Please, Olivia. Look at me. I'm telling you. The guy you think I am? That is who I am now.

OLIVIA. *(Unsure.)* OK …

ETHAN. Look, I could be anywhere right now. With just about anyone I wanted.

OLIVIA. *(A little stung.)* OK. Thanks for that.

ETHAN. No. I'm just saying, I'm here with you. I want to be here with you. And you have to know I wouldn't do anything to hurt you // or —

OLIVIA. How do I know that?

ETHAN. *(Exasperated.)* OK. So, you're going to trust … *(Pointing to the computer.)* *This* over me? Over who I am right here, standing right in front of you?

OLIVIA. *(Looking away, almost inaudible.)* … I …

ETHAN. *(After a moment.)* So, what? You want me to go?

OLIVIA. No. No. I … I *don't*.

ETHAN. So …

OLIVIA. So … *(After a moment.)* I just don't know what to do with all of this information. When I think about it … I …

ETHAN. So, don't think about it. *(Ethan moves in on her. Olivia is resistant but he doesn't give up. Their physical attraction slowly wins out and pulls them together. Clothes come off. Sex is imminent.)*

Scene 6

A week later. Late afternoon. Olivia is standing just inside the front doorway, her coat still on. Ethan sits in a chair, holding a book he's been reading.

OLIVIA. Even just talking about my writing again with someone like Susan would have been enough. But … she loved it.

ETHAN. I knew she would.

OLIVIA. And her response was so detailed and specific. Her reading was … very deep. And to be able to engage in that level of conversation about my work? I just … it was thrilling! I was terrified at first because, besides you, she's the only one who has read it. But hearing her talk about certain moments was so …

ETHAN. *(I get it.)* Yeah.

OLIVIA. I mean, she *loved* it.

ETHAN. I told you.

OLIVIA. You were right! I was so worried about dealing with the whole E. S. Thorn thing — that I'm getting all of this attention with this fictional biography — but she doesn't think it matters. She said me writing under E. S. Thorn might actually help us going forward — not sure how I feel about that — but she says we'll work it out.

ETHAN. Whatever they do, it'll be legal.

OLIVIA. Even if it's ethically sketchy?

ETHAN. She loved it. That's all you need to think about right now.

OLIVIA. She had some notes. But they actually didn't bother me. Her questions were very incisive and her thoughts were really smart —

ETHAN. What were her notes?

OLIVIA. She had some thoughts about the ending —

ETHAN. Yeah, she'll push you to change the ending.

OLIVIA. She wasn't suggesting that I change it // but that I think about —

ETHAN. She will. If you go with her. She will.

OLIVIA. Why?

ETHAN. Because it's not commercial. At all.

OLIVIA. So, what? You think she'll try and make it more commercial? I thought you trusted her?

ETHAN. As far as agents go, she's great. And you don't have to listen to her in the end. But she wants to make money. So, you should know if you sign with her, in the future, she's going to try and push you to be more commercial.

OLIVIA. Well, I'm not going to make any changes to my book that I don't believe in, but I liked what she had to say and I'm going to think about it.

ETHAN. OK. I'm just warning you.

OLIVIA. Why? Is that what happened to you? *Sex with Strangers* was really a warm, family drama until sneaky Susan got her hands on it?

ETHAN. I'm just saying, when they start talking about getting a deal and who wants what, it's easy to start compromising, to make money, to be *popular. (A text chime from Ethan's phone. He looks to it and reads as Olivia is talking.)*

OLIVIA. Yeah, well, I've been broke and obscure for so long, I'd be willing to compromise a little just to see what rich and popular is like. *(Re: his reading the text.)* Should I wait or…?

ETHAN. *(Texting now.)* I'm totally listening.

OLIVIA. OK. Well, I really don't think she's trying to make me compromise. I don't.

ETHAN. *(Back with her now.)* So, are you going to sign with her?

OLIVIA. I want to. If you're OK with it. The doors she could open for me … She said she'd take it to *FSG*.

ETHAN. FSG? Really?

OLIVIA. I know! She thinks they would really go for it.

ETHAN. FSG would be something.

OLIVIA. I know! They've published Flannery O'Connor! Roberto Bolaño! Jamaica Kincaid, Jeffrey Eugenides, Marilynne Robinson — it's crazy!

ETHAN. FSG. Fuck. *(After a moment.)* Yeah, well, those editors, they'll have some opinions. Susan's just an agent. But an editor at fucking FSG? You just better be ready for that.

OLIVIA. I am. It would be incredible to work with an editor on that level.

ETHAN. Sure. Maybe. But you give up a lot of control going somewhere like that.

OLIVIA. Is that true?

ETHAN. You really feel like you're going to have a leg to stand on with some editor who's worked with one of those writers? A house like FSG, if they really push you, would be great. But if they don't? Look, you're already established —

OLIVIA. Well, E. S. Thorn is established …

ETHAN. Your first book is selling incredibly well. It might be better to put the *new* one out yourself. *(Slowly, with a smile.)* Or …

OLIVIA. Or…?

ETHAN. Let me.

OLIVIA. What? Through your app, you mean?

ETHAN. Yes. You'd have total control. It could all happen *now*. You wouldn't have to go through the whole editing and galley process.

OLIVIA. Right. But … I, uh, I just, I want a real book.

ETHAN. Ebooks are real books.

OLIVIA. Right. But I want a deal that includes publishing a physical book. It won't feel real unless I can hold it in my hands.

ETHAN. You can pay to make one on-demand if a hard copy is so important.

OLIVIA. It's not the same.

ETHAN. But that's so … // old-fashioned …

OLIVIA. I know. But it's what I want.

ETHAN. All right. Well. It's great. Her being interested. It is. And possible deal with FSG? We'll see, but it's *great*.

OLIVIA. *(Unsure.)* OK. *(A text chime. Ethan looks to his phone.)*

ETHAN. Sorry. One second. *(Re: the email, shaking his head, smiling.)* Jesus.

OLIVIA. What?

ETHAN. Nothing. *(Putting his phone away.)* This guy's offering to pay me a crazy amount of money to go to his club opening in Vegas.

OLIVIA. And do what?

ETHAN. Nothing. Just to go.

OLIVIA. They're going to pay you to go to a party in Las Vegas?

ETHAN. Yeah. You know, celebrities go and cameras show up.

OLIVIA. *(Teasing him.)* Celebrities?

ETHAN. Whatever. It's stupid. But, it's *a lot* of money.

OLIVIA. So, you should go.

ETHAN. It's on Saturday and I'll be in LA then anyway.

OLIVIA. You will?

ETHAN. Yeah, I have to go back this weekend. There's this guy they want for the lead in the movie who I think just fucking sucks and we have to see him on Saturday because he starts shooting something in New Zealand or some shit on Monday. And if I'm not there to protest, it'll be him and the whole movie'll be fucked. So, I'll be out there but this party might be too cheesy, even for me. *(He turns his attention from the phone back to Olivia.)* Anyway, FSG! Susan! We should go celebrate.

OLIVIA. I'm not sure I feel like it now.

ETHAN. No, come on. Let's go out. We can go to that bar I was telling you about. You can meet some of my friends.

OLIVIA. I'm not up for *that* tonight.

ETHAN. Why?

OLIVIA. I don't want go to some hipster bar with your friends. I'll feel ... uncool.

ETHAN. OK. I'll tell them to meet us at the Olive Garden.

OLIVIA. Shut up.

ETHAN. And they're not all my age anyway. Ahmit for one.

OLIVIA. Did you tell him about us?

ETHAN. Yeah. I didn't think you'd care.

OLIVIA. No. I don't. But I'm not going out for a drink with you and Ahmit.

ETHAN. OK. Then, just me. Let's go to dinner. Somewhere really good.

OLIVIA. Somewhere really good?

ETHAN. Yeah. Wherever you want.

OLIVIA. OK. I want to go to that place where all the food is made into foam or cubes that taste like a full-course meal.

ETHAN. That's Willy Wonka's Chocolate Factory.

OLIVIA. No, you know what I mean — the crazy science food. Do you know what place I'm talking about?

ETHAN. I do.

OLIVIA. I think it's really expensive.

ETHAN. It is.

OLIVIA. Good! Let's go! I just have to change my shoes.

ETHAN. Can I borrow this one? *(Ethan picks up the book he was reading off the coffee table.)*

OLIVIA. *(Looking at the book.)* The Calvino? *Si si fantastico! (Olivia goes into the bedroom.)*

ETHAN. You know what else I looked at?

OLIVIA. *(Offstage.)* Snoop!

ETHAN. Besides your awesome vinyl collection …

OLIVIA. *(Offstage.)* That was my dad's. He had very good taste.

ETHAN. I looked at some of your old photo albums.

OLIVIA. *(Offstage.)* You didn't!

ETHAN. I did. *(Olivia returns carrying a different pair of shoes.)*

OLIVIA. That is incredibly unfair. One should be allowed to defend bad hairstyles of the past in person.

ETHAN. They weren't that bad, actually.

OLIVIA. *(Yes, they were.)* OK.

ETHAN. My mom has a bunch of picture albums from when I was a kid, but I don't have anything I can look through like that. I have it all on my computer.

OLIVIA. This is what I'm talking about. Soon, we won't have any of those objects anymore — no books, no photo albums, no records, tapes, even CDs — which were pretty soulless and awful — but now I feel nostalgic even about them. There'll be nothing to hold on to, put on a shelf. Nothing that lives with you in the world. We'll all live in empty white rooms, save for a couple of shiny silver rectangles that will hold our whole lives.

ETHAN. You make it sound so depressing.

OLIVIA. No, it's just … there are costs to all of this, you know? Things are lost. Things that were better. *(Ethan's phone buzzes. He looks to it. Touching her ears.)* Oh. Earrings. Be right there. *(Olivia exits to the bedroom. Ethan waits until she is gone.)*

ETHAN. *(Taking a moment, steeling himself for the call.)* OK. *(Answering the phone in full Ethan Strange mode.)* Dude! You fucking freak! Yeah, well, I'm a fucking *personality*! *(Darkly, an undercurrent of rage.)* Did she? Well, you'd better shut her up. I don't know. Give her the D. Let her choke on that … *(Olivia reenters, unseen by Ethan.)* No, I have too much going on. I know, dude, Vegas! *(Getting uglier and darker as he goes along.)* Yes, they were dirty, filthy, nasty little sluts, weren't they? Her name? There's only one thing I remember about her, brah, and I will tell you, it's not her name. Or her face. I know, man, what a fucking *night*!

Yeah. All right, we can talk about it but, right now, I gotta go. *(Olivia goes back into the bedroom, still unseen by Ethan, missing the rest of the conversation. Into phone.)* Yes. That *is* why, you dirty fucking dog. You know it! All right, dude, hit me later. *(Ethan hangs up. He shakes off the call, gathers himself. Olivia enters. He sees her. Back to himself.)* Ready to go, baby?

OLIVIA. Uh ... Yeah. Yeah. *(They move to the door.)*

Scene 7

A week later. An open suitcase sits on the floor. Olivia, still in her coat, stands looking at her iPad. Whatever she is looking at on the screen is making her very happy.

OLIVIA. *(With a smile.)* Yes. *(She goes to her computer, opens it, starts working. The buzzer sounds. She leaps up, presses the buzzer, opens the door, and sits back down. She notably suppresses the joy we just saw. After a moment, Ethan enters.)*

ETHAN. Hi.

OLIVIA. Hi.

ETHAN. It's really good to see you.

OLIVIA. You, too. *(Olivia goes to him. They kiss. She goes back to her computer.)*

ETHAN. Are you ready?

OLIVIA. Almost.

ETHAN. I thought you said seven.

OLIVIA. I did. Sorry. Traffic from the airport was awful and I just need a couple minutes.

ETHAN. *(Grumbly.)* OK. *(Ethan looks at Olivia's books.)*

OLIVIA. *(Changing the subject.)* So, what happened with the actor for your movie?

ETHAN. They're going with him.

OLIVIA. I'm sorry.

ETHAN. It's OK. It's hard not to take it personally, though. "Uh, yeah ... does the guy playing me have to be the biggest douchebag we saw?" "But, Ethan, man, he's just like you!" He's supposedly a massive draw with the demographic and blah, blah, fucking blah. *(After a moment.)* It's becoming clear to me that what they like is the *concept*, not my actual writing. And every suggestion they make keeps dumbing it down.

OLIVIA. But don't you have "sign off" or whatever it's called?

ETHAN. I'm supposed to but I've heard how these things go. I mean, I understand how they could see the idea as lowest common denominator, but the point is that I elevated it, right? The book is funny and smart and really well-written, but the way things are turning out, the movie's gonna be stupid and cheap.

OLIVIA. *(With good humor.)* Maybe you'll feel better if you go have a cry into your big bag of money.

ETHAN. *(With equal good humor.)* Maybe I will! I'm sure it'll be fine. *(His mood descending.)* But … they're really starting to treat me like I'm some kind of fucking novelty act.

OLIVIA. I'm sorry.

ETHAN. I wouldn't mind if it wasn't taking up all my time. I so want to be working on my app. We're supposed to launch in a week. But, right now, I need a drink. Come on.

OLIVIA. Three minutes. I really have to respond to this.

ETHAN. What's so urgent? Is it about the deal?

OLIVIA. Uh … yeah.

ETHAN. So, what? What did they say? Did FSG come in with the offer?

OLIVIA. Yes.

ETHAN. They did?

OLIVIA. They did.

ETHAN. I thought Susan was crazy to ask for that much. But they went for it?

OLIVIA. Yes.

ETHAN. *(Almost to himself.)* FSG. Fuck. *(Attention back to Olivia.)* You don't seem that excited.

OLIVIA. No. I am. There's just still a lot to figure out — you know, some of the terms …

ETHAN. But it's moving ahead?

OLIVIA. Yes. It is.

ETHAN. Well. Congratulations.

OLIVIA. Thank you.

ETHAN. *(Almost to himself.)* Fuck. Well … don't forget us philistines. *(Ethan looks to Olivia's bookshelves.)* Just think … in what? Eight months? You'll be on the shelf next to all your heroes. It's exactly what you wanted.

OLIVIA. …

ETHAN. What?

OLIVIA. *(Slowly.)* The deal.

ETHAN. Yeah?

OLIVIA. I'm … *(After a moment.)* I'm not exactly going to be on the shelf. They're starting a new division. Exclusively ebooks.

ETHAN. No.

OLIVIA. Yes. They want my book to launch it.

ETHAN. They're only going to do it as an ebook?

OLIVIA. Yes.

ETHAN. Then why are you doing that?

OLIVIA. It's *FSG*. They have big plans for me and about // how they're going to —

ETHAN. If they want it this badly, demand print. They are still a huge force in // the industry —

OLIVIA. We tried but they wouldn't go for it. The deal is contingent // on us agreeing —

ETHAN. So, fuck them. Put it out with someone who will give you the actual book you said you want.

OLIVIA. This is an incredible opportunity. And what it could lead to down the road? // It's —

ETHAN. I can't believe it. After all you've said about what you wanted, that you would actually agree to do it as an ebook —

OLIVIA. This is what I want now.

ETHAN. But if you don't care about the physical book, you don't need FSG. I'll put it out! There's no reason, now, I shouldn't. The launch of the app is going to be huge. But having you walk away from FSG and go with *me*? It would send a real signal. Of how serious what I'm doing is. It would be big.

OLIVIA. Ethan …

ETHAN. Do this. For me.

OLIVIA. Don't ask me that.

ETHAN. Have I asked you for anything?

OLIVIA. What do you mean?

ETHAN. For what I've done for you.

OLIVIA. Uh, no…?

ETHAN. So, do this for me.

OLIVIA. Why? Because I … *owe* you?

ETHAN. I'm just saying I was willing to do this before anyone else was in the picture.

OLIVIA. You're saying I owe you.

ETHAN. Well, don't you? Not in a bad way. And it's not like you'll be taking the hit in terms of money. I promise you'll make the same // as what you'd —

OLIVIA. You can't promise that. Look, Ethan, when this deal goes through, I'll be able to quit my job and write full-time. For *a couple of years.* You can't imagine what that means to me. What that could do for me.

ETHAN. I'll match their offer.

OLIVIA. What? No. I don't want you to —

ETHAN. Why not?

OLIVIA. It's not only about the money, Ethan. The more important thing, the *most* important thing is the association — to be associated with those FSG writers.

ETHAN. As opposed to being associated with me.

OLIVIA. I'm not saying that.

ETHAN. You are. You don't want to be associated with me.

OLIVIA. No. I don't want to be associated with *Ethan Strange.* Come on, it's not like you think your book is a masterpiece.

ETHAN. No, but what I'm working on — // what I'm doing —

OLIVIA. Look. I know you're trying to do something else, Ethan. I do. And that's great. But at this point, what you've put out into the world is mostly — *(Olivia stops herself before saying too much.)*

ETHAN. *(Quickly, pushing her.)* Is mostly *what?*

OLIVIA. Nothing.

ETHAN. What? *Shit?*

OLIVIA. No.

ETHAN. *(Quickly, pushing her hard.)* What?!

OLIVIA. *(Before she can stop herself.)* Irrelevant.

ETHAN. I can't believe you just said that to me.

OLIVIA. I'm sorry. I didn't mean — You know // what I'm —

ETHAN. Fuck you.

OLIVIA. Don't do that —

ETHAN. No. Seriously, fuck you. *(Ethan exits. She calls out the door after him to no avail.)*

OLIVIA. Ethan, please don't — ! You said yourself — ! *(To herself.)* Goddamnit! *(Lights.)*

Scene 8

Early the next morning. Olivia, still wearing some version of her outfit from the night before, is asleep on the couch. Her buzzer sounds. She wakes up but ignores it. It buzzes again. And again. And then, it doesn't stop.

OLIVIA. Asshole! *(Olivia presses the buzzer, waits for a second, then quickly fixes her hair. Ethan enters.)*

ETHAN. *(Very agitated.)* I know it's early. I did call. A thousand times. Your phone was off.

OLIVIA. It was on for a couple of hours. But, when I didn't hear from you, I turned everything off and fell asleep.

ETHAN. I'm sorry. But you said some really awful shit to me last night. And I was really fucking mad.

OLIVIA. I know.

ETHAN. And I ... I just have to talk to you right now.

OLIVIA. OK.

ETHAN. I, uh ... something happened.

OLIVIA. Oh, Ethan.

ETHAN. I, uh, I // went —

OLIVIA. Please don't. I really don't want to hear it.

ETHAN. Just let me // tell you —

OLIVIA. It's not like it hasn't crossed my mind — that it might not have *already* happened — what with all the pictures that keep surfacing —

ETHAN. What are you even talking about? // I'm trying to tell you —

OLIVIA. What I didn't expect is that it would only take one bad fight // for you to —

ETHAN. Wait — what do you think I did? You think I left here and hooked up with // some girl —

OLIVIA. Isn't that what you're // telling me?

ETHAN. You really trust me so little // that you think —

OLIVIA. I'm sorry. I don't know. I don't know what to think. Every week, there are these pictures of you // with these other girls!

ETHAN. What? Are you searching for these pictures?

OLIVIA. Sometimes.

ETHAN. Why?

OLIVIA. I don't know. Because I can, I guess.

ETHAN. Well, stop. Those pictures are old!

OLIVIA. Not the one last week, your trip to LA, the picture of that girl hanging all over you —

ETHAN. That was a stupid publicity thing! // She —

OLIVIA. Her tongue was in your mouth —

ETHAN. She grabbed me, kissed me, and the picture got taken.

OLIVIA. *(Unsure.)* OK …

ETHAN. It was two seconds of a stupid drunken kiss by some fat, dumbass, loser slut!

OLIVIA. Shut up! You don't know that girl. You don't know anything *about* that girl!

ETHAN. Why are we still talking about these girls?! They post these stupid pictures that mean nothing. They're writing about me, making up bullshit about me, *using* me to get attention for themselves. That's all it is.

OLIVIA. *(Sharply.)* I've heard you, Ethan. On the phone. Talking with your manager. You sound exactly like they describe you. Exactly like the guy in your books. It's not just pictures you can explain away.

ETHAN. When?

OLIVIA. What?

ETHAN. When have you heard me? Talking to my manager?

OLIVIA. I don't know.

ETHAN. I try and keep all of that bullshit away from you. So, unless you were listening in // on my conversations — ?

OLIVIA. Why do you do that? Unless you have something to hide?

ETHAN. For exactly this reason. I don't want you thinking — I told you, it's a character I'm playing.

OLIVIA. That is who you are, one-on-one, in private conversations. How can you tell me that's not you? How can I trust who you are right now?

ETHAN. Because Ethan Strange is over!

OLIVIA. He's not.

ETHAN. OK. Yeah. Another year or so. The movie'll get made, all the bullshit that goes with it. But quickly followed by the fast and final end of Ethan Strange. Until then? Yeah, you know … fuck. It is what it is. And, really, what's the harm?

OLIVIA. What's the harm? You're going to take all of *that* — what you say about women —

ETHAN. — not me! —

OLIVIA. And turn it into a movie that's basically a how-to guide for young men to treat women like garbage.

ETHAN. It's just a stupid movie!

OLIVIA. It's all so fucking awful!

ETHAN. It's fucking entertainment!

OLIVIA. To who? Not to me. It's not funny. It's // actually —

ETHAN. Well, a couple million people would disagree // with you.

OLIVIA. It's dangerous. It is.

ETHAN. I'm sorry if you're too old or too uptight to get it.

OLIVIA. And there it is.

ETHAN. You know, it's funny how all of it was *fine* with you as long as Ethan Strange was getting you an agent, getting you the exposure you wanted —

OLIVIA. That is a fucking outrageous thing to say —

ETHAN. Is it? You've known about the movie since I met you. Why the problem with it now? The truth is you've fucking hated me ever since you read my book. So, why have you stayed?

OLIVIA. Because! Because I thought you were this totally remarkable // person who —

ETHAN. At least I was honest.

OLIVIA. What?!

ETHAN. I told you from the first night what I did. But you, with your weak and helpless act, happy-in-your-obscurity bullshit —

OLIVIA. I never pretended to be anything but // what I am —

ETHAN. Covering this huge, raging ambition —

OLIVIA. Why am I not allowed to be ambitious?!

ETHAN. Why have you stayed? You hate me so much —

OLIVIA. I don't hate you! I stayed because // I actually —

ETHAN. You wanted to make sure you got your book deal.

OLIVIA. What?!

ETHAN. You made sure it was all worked out. You accepted their offer last night, didn't you?

OLIVIA. Yes. // But —

ETHAN. Turns out, you're just like all the rest of those girls, ready and willing to fuck me to get what you want.

OLIVIA. I can't // believe you —

ETHAN. The deal is done and here we are. How convenient is that?

OLIVIA. I didn't go with your app like you wanted and here we are. How convenient is *that*?

ETHAN. *(To himself.)* Fuck! *(To Olivia, slowly.)* My app launched last night … with the exclusive release of your new book.

OLIVIA. No. You … you didn't. You couldn't have!

ETHAN. I was going to show you what I could do. How much business I could generate // for you —

OLIVIA. But that's insane! What did you think // I would —

ETHAN. I knew it was stupid right after it went up. I took your book off right away.

OLIVIA. Did anyone get it?

ETHAN. A couple.

OLIVIA. So it's out there now?

ETHAN. Yeah.

OLIVIA. This could cost me everything — with FSG! With Susan! Everything!

ETHAN. I did it before I could even think about it. The things you said to me were so — but I'm sorry. I am. If there's anything I can do —

OLIVIA. Make this not be happening! Put the genie back in the bottle!

ETHAN. I'm sorry.

OLIVIA. How did you get it? I never gave you a copy. You stole it from me?!

ETHAN. I didn't take it to — I wanted to have it, but only for me.

OLIVIA. When did you take it?

ETHAN. Does it matter?

OLIVIA. When!

ETHAN. In Michigan. When I copied the first one. But, really, I only wanted to have it for me. Just for me.

OLIVIA. You need to go.

ETHAN. I never would have …

OLIVIA. Get out. Now.

ETHAN. *(Walking to the door.)* I don't expect you to forgive me. I just wanted to be the one to tell you.

OLIVIA. In my heart, I really didn't think you were that guy. At least not anymore. I am so incredibly stupid. *(Ethan walks out the door, but doesn't close it behind him. Olivia stands, stunned. After a moment, Ethan returns.)*

ETHAN. Olivia. What did you really think of my writing? Not the stories, but my *actual writing*.

OLIVIA. Honestly?

ETHAN. Yeah.
OLIVIA. *(Strongly.)* I thought it was ... fine.
ETHAN. Yeah. *(Lights.)*

Scene 9

A year and a half later. Summer. Evening. There are a few improvements/upgrades to the apartment/her stuff, and a dry cleaning bag with a couple men's shirts hang on the door to the bedroom or on a coat rack by the door. A FedEx package with a manuscript in it is on the coffee table. Olivia enters her apartment. Ethan walks in behind her, a nervous, cheery energy between them.

ETHAN. I buzzed, but when you weren't here —
OLIVIA. How long were you waiting?
ETHAN. Not that long.
OLIVIA. Why didn't you just call?
ETHAN. I was in the neighborhood.
OLIVIA. I didn't know you were in town. The Twitterverse usually announces your visits.
ETHAN. I came back to find an apartment.
OLIVIA. You're moving back?
ETHAN. Yeah. I thought about New York. But I just want to come home. LA sucked.
OLIVIA. Can I get you anything?
ETHAN. No, I'm good.
OLIVIA. So, the movie did all right.
ETHAN. All right enough to not be a liability, I hope. But not all right in any other way, really.
OLIVIA. I didn't see it.
ETHAN. I'm glad you didn't.
OLIVIA. That bad?
ETHAN. Worse than you can imagine, I think. *(A beat.)* You look great.
OLIVIA. Thanks. You, too. I had the big birthday.
ETHAN. Yeah, I know. I almost sent you something.

OLIVIA. You did?

ETHAN. Yeah, but, I thought it would be weird.

OLIVIA. *(After a moment.)* I kept waiting for you to write something about me. But you never did.

ETHAN. No. I figured I owed you that. *(After a moment.)* So, you're doing great. Your book's done so well.

OLIVIA. It's no *Sex with Strangers* but yeah. It also just got optioned for a movie, if you can believe it.

ETHAN. Really? That's great.

OLIVIA. Some twenty-two year-old starlet's company. They'll probably never make it … *(Olivia's phone buzzes. She looks to it. She puts down the phone.)* But still …

ETHAN. I'm so relieved that it all turned out all right.

OLIVIA. I bet. I kept thinking that if it didn't happen like it did — all the press about it, all the details of you and me, me being E. S. Thorn — it was *exactly* what I didn't want to happen, attention for all the wrong reasons. It was awful.

ETHAN. Yeah.

OLIVIA. *(With a smile.)* But it really did help sell the book. It helped a lot.

ETHAN. It did.

OLIVIA. I've often wondered if that's why you did it — you knew the shit-storm from the scandal would do more for me than anything the marketing department at FSG ever could.

ETHAN. Thanks for *thinking* that.

OLIVIA. It made me hate you less. Sometimes.

ETHAN. I'm glad. And thanks for not suing me.

OLIVIA. My lawyer will never get over it. But I figured I owed you that.

ETHAN. I don't know that you did.

OLIVIA. *(After a moment.)* I got the copy you made for me.

ETHAN. I didn't make // you a copy —

OLIVIA. Susan told me it was you.

ETHAN. Oh. She wasn't supposed to.

OLIVIA. She hates you, too, you know.

ETHAN. Oh, I know. I lost Susan, you and most of the writers on my app — all in a week. It was brutal.

OLIVIA. Yeah. *(After a moment.)* But, you were right.

ETHAN. Yeah?

OLIVIA. I was really sad I couldn't hold my book in my hands, couldn't put it on a shelf. I'm happy to have it.

ETHAN. Good. *(After a moment.)* Ahmit said you're getting married.

OLIVIA. Oh, uh, no. He's a good guy, a teacher. He just moved in. But we're talking about it, getting married …

ETHAN. That's great.

OLIVIA. Soon, probably. We want to have a kid and time is … you know.

ETHAN. You never told me that.

OLIVIA. Why would I? So you could run away screaming? I knew that wasn't anything you were interested in.

ETHAN. *(Flatly, his meaning unclear.)* Right. *(Ethan picks up the open FedEx envelope off the coffee table and removes the manuscript.)* So, you got it.

OLIVIA. Yeah. I did.

ETHAN. *(After a moment.)* So … what do you think?

OLIVIA. It just got here a couple of days ago.

ETHAN. You didn't read it?

OLIVIA. *(Slowly.)* No. I did.

ETHAN. And…?

OLIVIA. *(Slowly, getting emotional.)* And. I think … I think it's really quite … brilliant.

ETHAN. You do?

OLIVIA. I do. It's poetic and haunting and … very moving.

ETHAN. You sound a little shocked.

OLIVIA. I am.

ETHAN. *(A knife in the ribs.)* Oh.

OLIVIA. *(Slowly, still emotional.)* I'm sorry, but … I didn't know you could do … *that*.

ETHAN. *(After a moment.)* I haven't even given it to my new agent yet. It's so different from my other books, obviously. I'm going to put it out under a different name.

OLIVIA. Yeah?

ETHAN. I can't put it out as Ethan Strange because those readers will buy it and hate it and hate me for writing it. And the people who would like it won't buy it with that name on it …

OLIVIA. Any ideas?

ETHAN. Not yet. I've googled about a thousand names, but nothing I like comes back without all kinds of *stuff* attached.

OLIVIA. How about Cat Lunt?

ETHAN. *(Smiling.)* I bet that's still available. I'm thinking I'll just go with plain old Ethan Kane. *(After a moment.)* If I didn't meet you. Know you. I wouldn't have been able to. To write it.

OLIVIA. Well, I'm glad you finally did.

ETHAN. *(After a moment.)* How much of it, of our being together, was just about me do you think? Not what I made happen but just about … me?

OLIVIA. I don't know.

ETHAN. Wow.

OLIVIA. No. A lot. A lot of it. *(After a moment.)* How much of it was just about me?

ETHAN. A lot.

OLIVIA. Yeah.

ETHAN. *(After a moment.)* Come to dinner with me.

OLIVIA. No. I can't.

ETHAN. No funny business, I promise.

OLIVIA. Really, I can't.

ETHAN. Just a drink, then.

OLIVIA. Why?

ETHAN. I don't know. *(A beat.)* It just seems so unfair.

OLIVIA. What?

ETHAN. Your book made me love you. My book made you hate me.

OLIVIA. That's not …

ETHAN. I know. *(A beat.)* If only we could have met like two regular strangers. Sit at a bar. Talk. Get to know each other.

OLIVIA. It's too late. It's so too late.

ETHAN. But what if we're actually supposed to be together?

OLIVIA. What does that mean?

ETHAN. I don't know. *(Ethan slowly moves in on her.)*

OLIVIA. Ethan … *(He kisses her. She kisses him back, then stops herself.)* You should go. *(He walks to the door.)*

ETHAN. That bar on the corner, I'm just going to go sit there, have a couple of drinks. So, if you want, I'll be there.

OLIVIA. *(With finality.)* It was good to see you, Ethan.

ETHAN. Yeah. You, too. *(Ethan exits, leaving the door open. Olivia looks after him. After a moment of consideration, she grabs her bag and walks towards the door. She stops in the doorway. She turns around and steps back into her apartment. She turns again and steps back into the doorway looking after Ethan. Lights.)*

End of Play

PROPERTY LIST

Unbound manuscript
Red pen
Bottle of red wine
Wineglasses
Bag
Bowl of cereal
Juice glass
iPhone
Coffee
Small suitcase
Computer (laptop)
Computer (laptop, outdated)
Flash drive
iPad mini
Dry-cleaning bag with men's shirts
FedEx package with manuscript inside

SOUND EFFECTS

Car approaching
Car turning off
Peeing
Door closing
Toilet flush
Sounds of the city
Buzzer

NEW PLAYS

★ **AGES OF THE MOON by Sam Shepard.** Byron and Ames are old friends, reunited by mutual desperation. Over bourbon on ice, they sit, reflect and bicker until fifty years of love, friendship and rivalry are put to the test at the barrel of a gun. "A poignant and honest continuation of themes that have always been present in the work of one of this country's most important dramatists, here reconsidered in the light and shadow of time passed." –NY Times. "Finely wrought…as enjoyable and enlightening as a night spent stargazing." –Talkin' Broadway. [2M] ISBN: 978-0-8222-2462-4

★ **ALL THE WAY by Robert Schenkkan. Winner of the 2014 Tony Award for Best Play.** November, 1963. An assassin's bullet catapults Lyndon Baines Johnson into the presidency. A Shakespearean figure of towering ambition and appetite, this charismatic, conflicted Texan hurls himself into the passage of the Civil Rights Act—a tinderbox issue emblematic of a divided America—even as he campaigns for re-election in his own right, and the recognition he so desperately wants. In Pulitzer Prize and Tony Award–winning Robert Schenkkan's vivid dramatization of LBJ's first year in office, means versus ends plays out on the precipice of modern America. ALL THE WAY is a searing, enthralling exploration of the morality of power. It's not personal, it's just politics. "…action-packed, thoroughly gripping… jaw-dropping political drama." –Variety. "A theatrical coup…nonstop action. The suspense of a first-class thriller." –NY1. [17M, 3W] ISBN: 978-0-8222-3181-3

★ **CHOIR BOY by Tarell Alvin McCraney.** The Charles R. Drew Prep School for Boys is dedicated to the creation of strong, ethical black men. Pharus wants nothing more than to take his rightful place as leader of the school's legendary gospel choir. Can he find his way inside the hallowed halls of this institution if he sings in his own key? "[An] affecting and honest portrait…of a gay youth tentatively beginning to find the courage to let the truth about himself become known." –NY Times. "In his stirring and stylishly told drama, Tarell Alvin McCraney cannily explores race and sexuality and the graces and gravity of history." –NY Daily News. [7M] ISBN: 978-0-8222-3116-5

★ **THE ELECTRIC BABY by Stefanie Zadravec.** When Helen causes a car accident that kills a young man, a group of fractured souls cross paths and connect around a mysterious dying baby who glows like the moon. Folk tales and folklore weave throughout this magical story of sad endings, strange beginnings and the unlikely people that get you from one place to the next. "The imperceptible magic that pervades human existence and the power of myth to assuage sorrow are invoked by the playwright as she entwines the lives of strangers in THE ELECTRIC BABY, a touching drama." –NY Times. "As dazzling as the dialogue is dreamful." –Pittsburgh City Paper. [3M, 3W] ISBN: 978-0-8222-3011-3

DRAMATISTS PLAY SERVICE, INC.
440 Park Avenue South, New York, NY 10016 212-683-8960 Fax 212-213-1539
postmaster@dramatists.com www.dramatists.com

ML   8/2016